T0094757

Catching the Thread

Catching the Thread

Sufism, Dreamwork, & Jungian Psychology

LLEWELLYN VAUGHAN-LEE

THE GOLDEN SUFI CENTER

First published in the United States in 1998 by
The Golden Sufi Center
P.O. Box 456, Point Reyes, California 94956.

Fourth printing 2022.

Cover illustration by Tennessee Dixon.
Printed and bound in the USA

Library of Congress Cataloging-in-Publication Data:
Vaughan-Lee, Llewellyn.
[Call and the echo]
Catching the thread : Sufism, dreamwork & Jungian psychology / by Llewellyn Vaughan-Lee.
p. cm.
Includes bibliographical references and index.
Originally published: Putney, Vt. : Threshold Books, 1992.
ISBN 1-890350-00-1 (pbk.)
1. Spiritual life. 2. Dreams—Religious aspects. 3. Sufism.
I. Title.
BL624.V38 1998
297.4' 01' 9—dc21 97-38191
CIP

ISBN 13: 978-1-890350-00-0

CONTENTS

FOREWORD

Mysticism cannot be explained or comprehended by the mind. It belongs to another dimension, the dimension of the soul. Yet in *Catching the Thread* Llewellyn Vaughan-Lee has been able to describe many of the psychological and spiritual processes experienced by the seeker, the vicissitudes, the ups and downs, the slow progress on the path to the Real. He shows deep comprehension of the relationship with the teacher. In particular he has described one important event that is hardly mentioned in the great spiritual literature of the world: the union of the soul of the trainee with the soul of the teacher when the former has reached the required level of spiritual evolution. This event is a great mystery; perhaps the analogy of salt when it is dissolved in a glass of water comes nearest to describing it. Using dreams to illustrate the inner happenings of the soul, *Catching the Thread* describes the mysteries of the path in clear, contemporary language that must be specially helpful to the modern seeker.

Irina Tweedie

INTRODUCTION

Dreamwork is the modern equivalent of the ancient Sufi teaching stories.

Irina Tweedie[1]

Spiritual life is a response to a call. Of our own accord we would never turn away from the world and begin the long and painful journey home. But Someone calls to us, calls to us from within the depths of our heart, awakening our own deepest longing. This call is like a golden thread that we follow, guiding us deeper and deeper within, always pointing to the beyond. It is both intimate and elusive, for it does not belong to the mind but to the deepest core of our being. We hear it most easily when the conscious mind is still, which can be in meditation or when we are surrounded by the beauty of nature. But it is often in dreams that this call can be heard most clearly. In our sleep, when the outer world vanishes, our innermost secret can speak to us and guide us on this most difficult journey.

Dreams are like mirrors in which we can see ourselves. They reflect back our hidden self, revealing the true face of our own nature. In our sleep we are shown the mysteries, the beauty, and the horror of our inner world. Through dreams we can get to know this strange and yet familiar land. And when we wake, our dreams can be a doorway through which we can walk back into this inner world, can step into the landscape of the soul.

It is through this inner landscape that the spiritual traveler must find his or her way. The spiritual quest takes us deep into the hidden places of the soul, across the rivers, mountains, and great oceans of the psyche. We in the West have for so long looked only at the outer world that we have forgotten that the greatest journey is within. It is inside us that the real beauty and mystery are to be found. In the words of St. Augustine:

> People travel to wonder at the height of the mountains, at the huge waves of the sea, at the long compass of rivers, at the vast compass of the ocean, at the circular motion of the stars, and they pass by themselves without wondering.

The path we must follow is within us and here, within the psyche, are the guides that can help us on this journey. These are the inner figures of wisdom, like the wise old man and woman, and the innocent, eternal child. These figures have long been waiting for us to turn to them and ask their help. They know the most direct path that will take us home, and in our dreams they come to meet us. Most often they speak to us in the ancient language of symbols and images. In order to make best use of their wisdom we need to learn this symbolic language of the soul. It is for this reason that Sufis have long valued the wisdom of dreams and sought to understand the meaning of their images.

Spiritual life is a process of inner transformation, in which the whole psychic structure of the seeker is altered. These changes begin deep within the unconscious, in the very roots of our being; often the conscious mind is the last to be affected. Like seeds planted deep within the earth, the spiritual processes slowly germinate and may take years to flower into consciousness. But through dreams we are told of these changes, of the wondrous alchemy of the psyche through which our inner darkness is turned into gold. If we listen to such dreams we will see our inner path unfold. From this listening we can gain encouragement and also learn to live in harmony with these inner processes. If our conscious mind knows something of what is happening in the depths, we are then able to cooperate as fully as we can and not interfere with this mysterious but highly dynamic unfolding.

Modern psychology is invaluable, for it provides a language in which we can discuss and understand the processes of inner transformation. In particular, the work of Carl Jung and the school of Jungian psychology offers the most detailed exploration of the psychological dynamics experienced on the spiritual path. Before the advent of Jungian psychology, it was the alchemists who, within our Western culture, most fully described these processes. What the alchemists were working with in their retorts and crucibles were the projected contents of their own unconscious, and the symbolic and often paradoxical nature of alchemical texts reflects the irrational world of the psyche. Jung rediscovered the inner nature of the alchemical *opus* and translated the ancient wisdom of the alchemists into the language of psychology. Through his integration of the alchemical tradition with his own personal experiences of the unconscious, he charted a map of the unconscious that provides the contemporary seeker with a firm foundation for understanding what is happening within the psyche.

Sufism has always stressed the importance of the psychological aspects of the inner journey. Psychological work is a necessary preliminary stage on the path, in particular the work on the shadow, the purification of our lower nature and inner darkness. The processes of psychological integration and purification create an uncontaminated inner space within which the wayfarer can come to know the secrets of the soul, the deep mysteries of the heart. However, the language and terminology of most Sufi psychological treatises belong to a different culture from that of the Western seeker, and these works are not easily accessible. Integrating Jungian psychology within the framework of the Sufi path gives the wayfarer a valuable tool to work with in order to understand the psychological transformations on the path: how the darkness of the shadow is confronted and transformed, how our inner partner comes to meet us and helps us on the journey, how the Self arises from the unconscious and through its symbols reveals our primordial wholeness, the power and beauty of our innermost nature.

Yet, at the same time, many aspects of the path cannot be understood from a solely psychological perspective. The wayfarer seeks to journey far beyond the ego, even beyond the boundaries of the psyche. On this path leading to the Infinite, a psychological approach needs to be integrated with a spiritual perspective, and this is particularly important in dreamwork. While some dreams can be understood from a purely psychological standpoint, seekers often have dreams that require a spiritual context, an understanding of the nature of the journey that leads to love's infinite ocean. Some dreams not only have a personal meaning to the dreamer but, like myths or fairy tales, tell us about the archetypal nature of this quest. As with the Sufi stories of old, discussing these dreams can help us to become familiar with the mysterious ways of the heart and help us to find and follow the almost invisible thread that leads us home.

THE FOOLS OF GOD

The sect of lovers is distinct from all others;
Lovers have a religion and a faith all of their own.

Rûmî[1]

Beyond the Mind

Sufis are His most beloved fools, for He has a special tenderness for those who are lost in love. We talk of being madly in love with a human lover, but those who have been embraced by a divine lover are lost in a deeper madness, which is at the same time a secret so intimate that it can hardly be told in words. Love can never be understood by the mind. Those who wish to enter this path must accept that they can never explain either to themselves or to others the mysterious inner unfolding that is taking them home. The dynamics of the heart follow laws so different from those of the mind that the seeker needs to begin by accepting the mind's limitations, and realize that on the spiritual journey rational thought is a hindrance rather than a help. In the words of 'Attâr, "When love comes, reason disappears. Reason cannot live with the folly of love; love has nothing to do with human reason."[2]

The thinking processes of the mind have been developed to help us live in this physical world. They are very important for learning to drive a motor car or writing out a shopping list. But from a spiritual perspective, the mind is a limitation. It is known as "the slayer of the Real," for it stands between the seeker and the Real Self, while its constant chatter deafens us to our inner voice. The mind belongs to this world of duality. It understands through comparison. If you look at the workings of the mind you see that it is constantly comparing (Today is warmer than yesterday, but there is more wind than usual...). The mind is always caught between the opposites, their opposition largely created by the mind. As Prince Hamlet remarks, "there is nothing either good or bad, but thinking makes it so."[3]

Spiritual truth embraces rather than separates the opposites. Truth is not on the level of duality, but the experience of oneness. It is not found in the mind but in the heart, and on the path the wayfarer is thrown beyond the mind into a world that can be explained only in paradoxes. As the rational mind tries to assimilate experiences that belong to a different level of reality, the seeker is constantly left in a state of confusion. In the Sufi classic, *The Conference of the Birds*, 'Attâr tells the story of how a man's encounter with the path results in bewilderment, robbing him of both his possessions and his mind through the simple word "Enter."

> An Arab once went to Persia and was astonished at the customs of the country. One day he happened to pass the dwelling of a group of [dervishes] and saw a handful of men who said not a word. They had no wives and not even an obol, but they were pure of heart and undefiled. Each held a flask of muddy wine which he carefully filled before sitting down. The Arab felt sympathetic towards these men; he stopped and at that moment his mind and heart fell onto

the road. At this the [dervishes] said: "Enter, O man of nothing!" So he went in, willy-nilly, just like that! He was given a cup of wine and at once lost his senses. He became drunk and his strength was reduced to nothing. His gold and silver and valuables were taken from him by one of the [dervishes], more wine was given to him, and at last they put him out of the house. Then this Arab returned to his own country, one-eyed and poor, his state changed and his lips dry. When he arrived at his native place his companions asked him: "What is the matter? What have you done with your money and valuables? Were they stolen while you slept? Have you done badly in Persia? Tell us! Perhaps we can help you!"

"I was moving about in the street," he said, "when I fell in with a group of [dervishes]. I know nothing else except that my possessions and I were parted and now I have nothing." They asked him to describe the [dervishes]. He replied, "They simply said to me 'Enter.'"

The Arab remained ever after in a state of surprise and astonishment, like a child, and dumbfounded by the word "Enter."

You too, put your foot forward. If you do not wish to, then follow your fantasies. But if you prefer the secrets of the love of your soul you will sacrifice everything. You will lose what you consider to be valuable, but you will soon hear the sacramental word, "Enter."[4]

The Subversion of the Mind

As the wayfarer travels along the path, the energies of the heart gradually subvert the thinking processes of the mind. Because the energy of love is more powerful than the mind, it secretly slows down the mind, until the mind becomes empty and thus able to experience the inner reality of the Self, which is love. The following dream illustrates this dynamic. It left the dreamer with an experience of love such as he had never known before:

> I was in a hall full of men on soapboxes, who were giving political speeches to groups of people around them. However, in the hall there was a small number of men who were subverting all this activity by giving out little slips of paper to people around them. Slowly the hall emptied of people and the men on soapboxes left. When the hall was empty, the five men who had been secretly subverting the whole process came together and there was such a feeling of love between them. I awoke filled with this feeling of love.

Our minds are so often like this dreamer's hall, full of men on soapboxes bombarding us with different opinions and ideas. To consciously confront this dynamic would only feed more energy into the mind, fill the hall with more people. The Sufi path is subversive rather than confrontational. It works from within, from the Self which lives in the very depths of the unconscious, in the secret recesses of the heart. The changes begin far away from the conscious mind, where they cannot be interfered with. Then slowly the energy of the Self filters into consciousness, where it begins the work of altering our thinking processes.

The spiritual dynamic is a process of being speeded up. To quote St. John, "It is the spirit that quickeneth,"[5] and as we travel along the path, we tune into, or are infused with, the higher frequency of our spiritual nature. The energy of the Self is far quicker than that of our physical or mental bodies. As we meditate and aspire we create a deeper bonding with our Higher Self which allows its quicker energy to be integrated into our consciousness. It is this energy which transforms us. In the dream of the men on soapboxes, slowly the people leave the hall and the room is left empty except for the five men who secretly instigated the process of subversion. The energy of the Self gradually speeds up consciousness and in so doing throws out the slower, denser thought patterns. Then, when the ordinary consciousness is empty, the individual is able to experience the inner reality of love. This is the dreamer's final experience; he tastes the substance of the Self.

This transformation is a gradual process because the inner energies are so powerful that the structure of consciousness needs to be attuned slowly in order to be able to integrate them. In the words of T. S. Eliot, "human kind cannot bear very much reality"[6]; this is because ordinary consciousness would simply be shattered by the higher vibrations of the Self. Our mental hospitals contain many people who have had an experience of an inner reality which their consciousness could not contain. Just a glimpse of our true nature is awe-inspiring, "awful." Sometimes, when an individual begins on the path, when he begins to meditate, he may be given such a glimpse. This can be an encouragement, but it can also be frightening, because it points beyond the ego and the mind, beyond the known into the unknown. Then a teacher is needed, one who is a few steps further along the way and speaking from experience can say: "No, you are not going mad. What you have experienced is not unusual. You have just touched an inner dimension that is very different from the external world. It is a good sign."

However, there can also come the time when the higher energies are necessary to shatter the rigid patterns of our ordinary consciousness, to break our self-imposed boundaries. This only happens when the teacher knows that the seeker is ready, usually after years of meditation and spiritual practices have silently prepared a new inner vessel. This inner work makes the seeker both finer and stronger, and thus allows him to live in the world of everyday consciousness and at the same time in tune with the inner dimension of the Self.

Such an experience of inner transition can be both dramatic and disturbing. It can be triggered by an outer situation or specifically by the teacher. Something happens, often a shock that throws the individual off balance. Sufi teachers often use shock tactics, even accusing the devotee of something totally unjust, to deliberately bring about this unbalancing. When our consciousness is totally "balanced" there is no space for the higher dimension to come through. As a Canadian psychiatrist observed:

> When a human being is standing with both feet firmly on the ground, with both legs on the earth, and is "quite normal" as we medical practitioners call it, spiritual life is very difficult, perhaps impossible. But if something is not

> quite right with the mind, a little wheel not working properly in the clockwork of the mind, then spiritual life is easy.[7]

When the mind is thrown off balance, the higher, faster energies are able to come through, and it is their vibrations that break up the barriers of consciousness, the patterns of conditioning. At this moment it is vitally important that the seeker surrender to the process, however painful or unjust it may seem. Yet, because the values of the Self are so different from those of the ego and the conscious mind, the seeker is presented with every reason to reject this process of inner destruction.

The values of the ego are a limitation, and for the sincere seeker the teacher or life itself will present the opportunities that will bring about both inner destruction and freedom—if they are unconditionally accepted. But in these situations of pain and inner panic, there is the danger that the seeker will try to hold onto the wreckage, to find some security in the patterns of the past, in parental or social conditioning. Bombarded by the energy of the Self, the wayfarer can find no security except in total insecurity; yet still the ego, frightened by the limitless horizons of the Self, clings to the world of reason and the limited values of the past. It clings to the wreckage of a ship that can no longer take us on any journey, and yet this wreckage prevents us from realizing that we can swim, naked and alone. In time the wreckage will decay or float away and the final result will be the same, but it will have been a longer and more painful journey. Spiritual life has its cycles and there are moments that must be grasped and totally surrendered to. Often these moments of greatest opportunity are disguised, appear "unspiritual" or cruel. It is said that the teacher puts all appearances against himself, and then tests the disciple. Life does the same. It is best never to reject what life brings, and often the most difficult circumstances hide something of infinite value. The light is hidden in darkness, but the darkness must be fully accepted before the light reveals itself. When the Sufi Abû Sa'îd ibn Abî-l-Khayr was asked what Sufism entailed he replied: "Whatever you have in your mind—forget it; whatever you have in your hand—give it; whatever is to be your fate—face it!"[8]

Khidr, the Green Man

We all have free will, and to surrender to a painful experience that can appear unjust, even cruel, is never easy. This is why Sufi teaching emphasizes the importance of unconditional surrender, surrender to the teacher and surrender to life. It shows how one can never judge by appearances, as in the following story of Khidr and Moses as told in the Qur'an:

> At the place where the two seas meet, Moses met Khidr, one whom Allâh had given knowledge of Himself. Moses asked Khidr, "May I follow you so that you may guide me by that which you have been taught?"
>
> "You will not be able to bear with me," Khidr replied. "For how can you bear with that which is beyond your knowledge?"
>
> Moses said, "If Allâh wills you will find me patient; I shall not disobey you in anything."

Khidr said, "If you want to follow me, you must not ask any questions about anything, until I myself speak to you about it."

The two set out. They embarked on a ship and immediately Khidr bored a hole in the bottom of the ship.

"What a strange thing you have done!" exclaimed Moses. "Have you bored a hole in order to drown the ship's passengers?"

"Did I not tell you," he replied, "that you would not bear with me?"

"Pardon my forgetfulness," said Moses. "Do not be angry with me because of this."

They continued on their journey until they met a young man. Moses' companion killed this young man, and Moses said: "You have killed an innocent man who has done nothing wrong. You have committed a wicked crime."

"Did I not tell you," Khidr replied, "that you would not bear with me?"

Moses said: "If I ever question you again, abandon me; for then I would have deserved it."

They journeyed on until they came to a certain city. They asked the people for some food, but these people would not receive them as guests. Finding a wall on the point of falling down, Moses' companion repaired it. Moses said to his companion, "If you had wanted, you could have asked payment for your work."

"The time has now come when we must separate," said Khidr. "But first I will explain to you the meaning of those acts which you could not bear to watch with patience.

"The ship belonged to some poor fishermen.

> I damaged it because if it had gone to sea it would have been captured by a king who was seizing every boat by force.
>
> "The young man was a criminal, who would have committed many crimes that would have brought sorrow to many people, including his parents.
>
> "As for the wall, it belonged to two orphaned boys in the city whose father was an honest man. Beneath the wall their treasure is buried. Allâh decreed in his mercy that they should dig out this treasure when they grew to manhood. What I did was not by my own will.
>
> "That is the meaning of my acts which you could not bear to watch with patience."[9]

Three times Moses judged Khidr by the appearance of his actions. Three times he failed to remain silent and accept that one to whom God had revealed Himself sees and acts from a different perspective. What Khidr did was not his will, but the will of Allâh. Moses represents the rational, outer law, the exoteric. Khidr, one to whom Allâh had revealed Himself, "endowed with knowledge of Our Own," represents the inner, esoteric path of the mystic. He is the archetypal figure of the Sufi saint, or *wali,* who has direct inner communion with the Absolute, and follows the inner law, the divine hint, regardless of outer appearances. The Sufi master, Bhai Sahib, stresses how one should never judge by appearances:

> Saints are like rivers; they flow where they are directed.... If a Hint is there, I have to do it, and if I don't, I am MADE to do it. Divine Hint

> is an Order. Sometimes the Saints have to do things the people will misjudge, and which from the worldly point of view could be condemned, because the world judges by appearances. One important quality required on the Path is never to judge by appearances. More often than not things look different from what they really are. There is no good or evil for the Creator. Only human society makes it so. A Saint is beyond good or evil, but Saints are people of the highest morality and will never give a bad example.[10]

The teacher may act with seeming coldness, even inhumanity, but he acts from the level of the Self. He follows the laws of a world very different from the physical plane and is concerned with the real freedom of the seeker, freedom from the ego and the duality of good and bad, just and unjust. In this world of illusion all that matters is our relationship with the Beloved. The eighth-century Sufi saint, Râbi'a, expresses this in her usual straightforward manner:

> O God! if I worship Thee in fear of Hell, burn me in Hell; and if I worship Thee in hope of Paradise, exclude me from Paradise; but if I worship Thee for Thine own sake, withhold not Thine everlasting beauty.[11]

While the religious man avoids evil and strives towards good, seeking a reward in heaven, the Sufi sees the opposites of heaven and hell as a limitation. Furthermore, there is a danger in performing good deeds for the sake of the hereafter:

> It would mean that the self would reappear on the higher level. We may plant a huge weed, and to eradicate it would be practically impossible.[12]

The wayfarer believes only in oneness and seeks the total annihilation of the ego. Inwardly he seeks to embrace and thus transcend the duality of good and evil; yet, as he travels along the path, he instinctively avoids actions that are morally bad, and tends towards the good. Evil is denser and slower than good, and as the wayfarer "speeds up" he is actually unable to enact evil. This does not happen through moral choice, which divides, but through a state of being.

The Sufi is interested in neither this world nor the next, in neither heaven nor hell. He will pay any price to reach Reality in this life. The price is that "everything has to go," and like any mental belief, the values of good and bad can be a limitation. Even the desire to renounce must be left behind. One Sufi poet wrote: "On the hat of poverty three renouncements are inscribed: 'Quit this world, quit the next world, quit quitting.'"[13]

Rather than being guided by the values and concepts of the mind, the seeker travels a path that leads to a natural state of being. As the mind is subverted, a different level of existence is experienced. This is imaged in the following dream:

> I am reading a book, but the light gets slowly dimmer and dimmer. I bring the light closer to the book, but finally the light goes out. The door opens and on the landing is an old lady with white hair. She beckons and I follow her

downstairs. The downstairs room is full of light. There are great trees growing in it.

Reading a book, the dreamer is following the conditioned wisdom of the world. But slowly this process grows more and more difficult, until "the light went out." Then, in this dark empty space, the wise old woman appears, representing the dreamer's inner wisdom. We have to reach a point of *unknowing*, an empty darkness, before we can realize our deeper knowing. The outer wisdom of the world will never take us home; we have to give it up, put down the book, before we can be led back to ourselves, back to our essence. Yet, as this dream images, the seeker does not actively renounce anything; rather what she needs to leave behind is taken away. The light, the attitude of consciousness with which she followed the outer wisdom, grows dimmer and dimmer and finally goes out.

The wise old woman is the dreamer's inner teacher, who is both her deepest wisdom and the guide who will take her there. Beckoning to the dreamer she leads her downstairs, away from the mind into the radiance of her own natural Self, the tree of life that images her own deepest unfolding.[14]

Dreams often amplify each other, describing the same central dynamic from different perspectives. The psyche is not a logical or linear dimension, but a fluid play of interrelationships whose meaning and significance are often best conveyed through a series of different scenes. A previous dream also led this dreamer to the same image of a tree, though in this dream it is a love affair that takes her there:

> I am a young Irish girl living with a family. I am in love with the son. I go into the room to see him and discover that he has a twin, although I hadn't known it before. They are lying on the bed and I look out of the window behind them. There is a beautiful man of glowing green, made of a tree or a tree made of him—branches come out of his fingers.

Looking for her lover, the dreamer discovers his twin, who she has never known existed. This image of the twin reflects an ancient tradition of the "heavenly twin": we each have our heavenly twin who lives in the world of light. This twin is invisible to the eyes of the senses, and is normally reunited with us only at death. The dying words of Mani, the founder of Manicheism, were, "I contemplated my Double with my *eyes of light*."[15]

In the Sufi tradition this heavenly twin is our "witness in heaven" *(shâhid fil-samâ)*, who sees with the eyes of God and thus sees our life from a spiritual rather than worldly perspective. He or she is interested only in the evolution of the soul and can appear at moments that are important for the spiritual direction of our life. This twin can manifest as an inner prompting, a dream, or even as an external figure. It is usually only afterwards that the importance of such a figure is recognized, as when Jesus appeared to the two disciples on the road to Emmaus. For the Sufi, Khidr is such an inner guide who often appears as an ordinary man. Only when he has gone does his transcendent nature become apparent.

The wayfarer is one who aspires to "die before he dies," and thus seeks to reunite with the heavenly twin while still living in this world, in this way forming a link between the two worlds and allowing the energy of the inner world to manifest on the physical plane. Irina Tweedie explains this process:

> It should be borne in mind that the function of the disciple is to focus a stream of energy of some special kind upon the physical plane where it can become an attractive center of force and draw to itself similar types of ideas and thought currents, which are not strong enough to live by themselves or to make a sufficiently strong impact upon human consciousness.[16]

It is due to the influence of her heavenly twin that the wayfarer becomes a "point of light," a light in which others will be able to see and recognize their own inner nature and come closer to their own true self.

In seeking her lover the dreamer discovers he has an unknown twin. Then, through the window, she sees "a beautiful man of glowing green, made out of a tree or a tree made out of him." This natural being is herself: in the words of Meister Eckhart, "the pure being that always was His and shall remain His eternally."[17] This green man is her heavenly twin seen in his own natural environment, in the world of the spirit.

Green is the color of nature, and it is also the color of the realization of God, the "Emerald Rock" which exists on the top of the mystical Sinai, the mountain "which the exile must climb when he is summoned at last to return *home*, to return *to himself*."[18] The figure of Khidr, the Green Man, is an archetypal symbol of our inner essence, and like the wise old man or woman is also the guide that reveals this secret:

> I am transcendent reality, and I am the tenuous thread that brings it very close. I am the secret of man in his very act of existing, and I am that invisible one who is the object of worship... I am the Shaikh with the divine nature, and I am the guardian of the world of human nature.[19]

I was once told in a dream that "only saints and animals are realists." Both saints and animals experience life directly without the prejudices of personality or the conflicts of the ego. They follow the natural law of their own being, which relates directly to the whole of life. Yet people who live according to their own inner nature are often a threat to others. Jung describes how he sometimes had this effect on others:

> I can imagine myself in many instances where I would become sinister to you. For instance, if life had led you to take up an artificial attitude, then you wouldn't be able to stand me, because I am a natural being. By my very presence I crystalize; I am a ferment.
>
> The unconscious of people who live in an artificial manner senses me as a danger. Everything about me irritates them, my way of speaking, my way of laughing. They sense nature.[20]

A Lover's Gift

It is said that Sufis are loved more than others and hated more than others. Love, which is the most natural power in the universe, is both creative and destructive. It destroys the patterns of the mind in order to give birth to the Self. Love is both the beginning and the end of the quest. It is a gift given by the Beloved, a gift whose beauty and intimacy are hinted at in the following dream:

> I am given as a gift a box. I open it and the inside is covered in red silk. In the middle of the box is a single hair.

There is a custom among lovers that the beloved gives a lock of her hair which the lover treasures above anything else. In Victorian times this lock of hair would be placed in a heart-shaped locket, or a ring. But the custom is much older; it appears in this twelfth-century Sufi poem by 'Attâr, in which the human beloved is a symbol for the Divine:

> If I could possess but one strand
> Of her tresses, I would treasure it
> As the heart's precious eye,
> As my soul's own foster love.[21]

The relationship of the lover and the Beloved is the core of the Sufi path. To quote Bhai Sahib: "In the whole of the universe there are only Two: the Lover and the Beloved."[22] At the beginning of the journey the Beloved may appear only as an abstraction, as an idea rather than a reality. But later the Beloved becomes an inner reality, more tender and intimate than a human lover can ever be.

However distant the Beloved may seem, He is always infinitely close—in the words of the Prophet, "closer to us than our jugular vein." He calls to us from within our own hearts, and it is only the mind and the ego that separate us. This relationship is so intimate because it is inward—"No one is more inward than I"[23]—always taking us deeper within our own being. It is for this reason it seems so personal, so unshareable, this relationship of essence to Essence. When Krishna was dancing with sixteen thousand milkmaids, each thought that he was dancing only with her. And because He, the Great Artist, created each of us unique, our relationship with Him will be unique, different for each of us. The essence of this relationship is the offering of our own individual self back to the Creator, an offering which is in its deepest sense an act of prayer: "Every being has his own appropriate mode of prayer and glorification."[24] For each seeker the spiritual path will be different, because each of us is different. Every lover makes his own unique pilgrimage within the heart. And He loves us each for our own individual self. He loves the fact that we are different because He made us different.

In this love affair there can be neither comparison nor competition. We each must find our own way of loving Him, of being with Him. The love affair with the Beloved is so inward that we will share ourselves with Him as with no outer lover. It is in this sense that a love affair with Him is easier than any other love affair. We know in our heart that He will never betray us. And just as we come naked to a human lover, we should come naked to the Beloved. Our clothes are our personality, conditioning, and attachments that separate us from Him who is our own deepest Self. When we are naked He can touch us more tenderly, be more intimate with us. "And the time will come when one wishes that twenty-four hours should be twenty-five in order to love someone one hour more."[25]

Poems of the Soul

The relationship with the Great Beloved does not belong to the ego or the personality. It is the love affair of the soul and the Source. The consciousness of the seeker experiences this intimate affair only through reflection: the drama of the heart is reflected into a mind refined and emptied through meditation and spiritual practices. But during the night, when the conscious mind is asleep, the heart is able to tell its story through the medium of dreams. Such dreams, like myths, are the poems of the soul, sometimes embracing a whole lifetime in a series of images. This is true of the following dream, which tells the inner story of the dreamer's life—"the past, the present, and the future":

> I enter a modern house and am amazed to discover that the interior is an ancient, Middle-Eastern palace, indescribably beautiful. I am summoned to the king and am his mistress, decked out in oriental finery, jewels and perfumes.
>
> Entering the king's bedchamber, I see him lying on the bed. He calls me to him and I climb in beside him. I know that this is the last time, for he is now old and impotent. He just wants me there to look at and to warm him. I am an object. Then a gust of wind blows from the door on the left towards me and the bed speaks. I am told that I must return everything that I have acquired in my life—my conditioning and attitudes, everything that I have stolen or has been thrust upon me by others, by my parents, etc.

One by one everything leaves me and returns from whence it came, and finally I am left standing completely naked.

Then the voice tells me that I am to be given gifts from the gods, the Olympians. Each of the gods is announced in turn. I am told the name of the god or goddess that has supplied it. These wonderful gifts clothe me inwardly not outwardly. I become full of light, and for the first time in my life, I look at my body and see it as beautiful, radiant and full of love. All my anxieties about being naked vanish, for I know that people will now only see the light or themselves reflected back.

Then I take the ring which the old king, my father, had given me. I untwist the four strands of silver wire, and there, to my amazement and wonder, I discover a fine, gold filament. I nearly didn't notice it because it was at first dull from being hidden for so long. As I hold it I tremble with the recognition that this is the hair that is the bridge across the chasm of fire. There is an overwhelming, indescribable feeling of love.

I am then magically transported to the bedchamber of the prince, whom I know that I am to marry. There is also the knowledge that he will soon be king and rule in place of the old order. I can feel his presence in the room but I do not see his face. He is waiting for me to join him.

I awoke from the dream with great feelings of excitement. I am going home. I am going home. But then on writing the dream down I am overtaken with tremendous grief, longing, and the feeling of painful separation. It is a dream of the past, the present, and the future.

The images of dreams have their own pattern which reflects the pattern of the soul. But their meaning can also be unfolded, the richness of their tapestry more fully understood. Such dreams can teach us about the inner processes of the psyche, pointing from the psychological dynamics of the past to the transformations that take us to the beyond.

The King's Mistress

In this dream the dreamer enters the house of her own psyche, to discover that behind its modern facade is an ancient and "indescribably beautiful" inner world, imaged as a Middle-Eastern palace. This is the fairy-tale world of the soul, where we are all kings and queens, princes and princesses, and also wizards and witches. Our dreamer is the mistress of the king and wears the jewels and perfumes of a woman of pleasure. The king is the ruling masculine principle in the dreamer's life, and later in the dream he is associated with her father and the world of her conditioning. From our parents we inherit not just our physical features, but also our attitudes and outlook on life. Their values become our values, and the fact that the dreamer is the king's mistress indicates the way the dreamer allows her true femininity to be used for another's pleasure. She suffers the collective plight of the feminine made subservient by centuries of patriarchal pressure. Many women of today, even the most strident feminists, prostitute their inner goddess on the altars of a male-dominated culture. For behind the pressure that has made women subservient to men lies an inner and more powerful dynamic: the repression of the feminine principle itself. The inner wisdom and creative mystery of the feminine have been buried and forgotten, and only the external goals of the masculine remain.

Entering the bedchamber of the king, the dreamer plays the part of the mistress. But the inner dynamic has changed, for she knows that he is old and impotent, and "this is the last time." The old and impotent king is a powerful mythic image, best known in the Grail legend of the Fisher King. In the story of the Fisher King, the wounding and impotence of the king have resulted in his kingdom's becoming a wasteland. In our dream the wasteland motif is suggested in the dreamer's awareness that she is just "an object." To be "an object" in a relationship is a denial of that which is most precious: one's own individual self. As "an object" one cannot experience real relating, only a sense of inner desolation. If the individual is not valued, she becomes neglected and forlorn. Without a real exchange there can be no creativity; nothing can be born. And just as this is true on the outer stage of human relationships, it is also true of the inner dynamic within the psyche. The inner and outer mirror each other. The king's impotence is the inability of the dreamer's conditioning to relate to her real self. Because of this, while the king remains in power there can be no inner growth.

It is often only when a cycle is ending that we become fully conscious of its dynamic. In bed with the king for the last time, the dreamer realizes that she is only an object to him. She sees the sterility of their relationship, and then a gust of wind blows from the left, and her inner life changes forever. The wind is always the wind of the spirit, and this spiritual force that blows away the past comes from the left, from the unconscious. The seeds of inner change lie buried deep within the psyche, hidden from the light of consciousness. In the innermost chamber of the heart the Real Gardener tends these seeds, for they are the seeds of His own unfolding. There they germinate and grow, until finally they force themselves into consciousness, and He begins to reveal Himself.

With the wind comes a voice from the bed, the place of her surrender to the king. In a dream a disembodied voice is usually the voice of the Higher Self, and here the voice tells her to return everything that she has acquired in her life: "my conditioning and attitudes, everything that I have stolen or has been thrust upon me by others, by my parents, etc." We are born into this world both physically and psychologically naked, but only too soon are we clothed in the values of the world, burdened by our conditioning, imprisoned by the desires of the ego. Spiritual life requires that we free ourselves of these burdens. To quote Bhai Sahib: "You come naked into the world and you go naked. When you come to the Spiritual Teacher, you have to be naked!"[26]

You can only approach the spiritual path as your true self, and much of the inner work that prepares the seeker for the path is a process of stripping away all the layers of conditioning that hide and protect us from ourselves. This dream describes a secret of this nakedness. Only when we are naked and vulnerable are we able to receive the gifts of the spirit; only when our outer coverings are removed can we realize our deeper inner qualities. These inner gifts come from the archetypal world of the soul, which the Greeks projected onto the gods of Olympus. They can include the joyous ecstasy of Dionysus, the dark wisdom and healing powers of Hecate, the homemaking warmth of Hestia, or the valor of Ares. The gifts of the gods are many and bountiful, and we all have our share. But mostly they are hidden beneath the shadows of our personal psyche. In our nakedness, our archetypal essence shines. It is a light in which we can see our own beauty more clearly: "I become full of light and for the first time in my life I look at my body and see it as beautiful, radiant and full of love."

The Divine Beauty of the Feminine

Uncovered, we become what we really are: luminous and beautiful beings. We are made in the image of That Which Is The Source Of All Light, The Origin Of All Beauty. Each human being is a unique manifestation of His light, a unique reflection of His beauty. And a part of the mystery of the creation is that the feminine principle of matter embodies these qualities. In discovering her deeper Self, a woman has access to this mystery and can realize the divine beauty of her own body. Aphrodite's gift of beauty belongs to every woman, for it is an inner experience made manifest. In ancient times, in the ritual bathing and adornment of their bodies, the priestesses honored the Goddess, the feminine side of God. Such rituals remain in a woman's enjoyment of perfumes or in the attention she may pay to her hair. An adolescent girl's preparation for a party can have the quality of an initiation rite, for in the deepest sense she is not just making herself attractive to others but honoring the goddess archetype.

> The woman conscious of the goddess cares for her body with proper nutrition and exercise and enjoys the ceremonies of bathing, cosmetics and dress. This is not just for the superficial purpose of personal appeal, which is related to ego gratification, but out of respect for the nature of the feminine. Her beauty derives from a vital connection to the Self.[27]

Yet, with the repression of the feminine, the sacredness of this mystery has been abused; this connection with the Self has been almost lost. Just as the dreamer adorned herself with finery and jewels for the pleasure of the king, so has the beauty of the feminine body been prostituted for the pleasure of men. Women have learned to value themselves in relation to men rather than in relation to their inner selves.

In returning the clothes of her conditioning, the dreamer is able to discover, to see "for the first time," the real nature of her body's beauty, which is that it is "radiant and full of love." Love is the substance of the Self, and beauty is love made manifest. When a woman is in love she is at her most beautiful. She is radiant. But most radiant is she who is in love with the Beloved. She is then clothed with the fabric of love:

> For where your treasure is, there will your heart be also.
>
> The light of the body is the eye: if therefore thine eye be single, thy whole body shall be full of light....
>
> And why take ye thought for raiment? Consider the lilies of the field, how they grow; they toil not, neither do they spin.
>
> And yet I say unto you, That even Solomon in all his glory was not arrayed like one of these.[28]

The Beloved wants us as we really are, and because in the core of our being we know this, we long to be naked before Him. In becoming naked we come to know our real nature, and then one of the great spiritual mysteries is revealed: what we find under our own clothes is none other than He. As Muhammad said: "He who knows himself knows his Lord." The deeper we go within, the more clearly we realize that there is no separation, no duality, that the Creator and the creation are one. It is only because of the coverings of the ego that we ever experience separation. In the words of the Sufi poet, Hâfiz: "Between the lover and the beloved there must be no veil. Thou thyself art thine own veil, Hâfiz—get out of the way!"[29]

Spiritual nakedness is our deepest and most natural state. And while the act of undressing—of taking off the clothes of this world—may require considerable effort, nakedness is an effortless state. It is a state of being. The seeker works with all her energy to remove her coverings, to polish the mirror of the heart. Then in the clear surface of this mirror she can see her own essence reflected: the face she had before she was born. In this mirror she can see her own light, which is also the light of her Beloved's eyes. This glance is a gift, and it is not given to the seeker alone. The mirror of the heart reflects upon all who look. In the story "The Emperor's New Clothes" the king's nakedness reflects the stupidity and ignorance of those who see him. Only the innocent child sees the truth: that the emperor has no clothes on. Spiritual nakedness also reflects, but in wisdom, not ignorance. Those who look can see both their own beauty and their blemishes. They can see behind the coverings of the persona to the deeper layers of both light and darkness. In just being herself the wayfarer has a dynamic effect upon others: they are able to see themselves as they really are.

The anxieties of the dreamer vanish when she realizes that people will not see her nakedness but "only the light or themselves reflected back." Then, in her new-found nakedness she is able to take off the last article from the past: "the ring which the old king had given me." At this moment in the dream she realizes that the old king is her father. As her father's mistress she was caught within the Oedipus complex, the primary stage of sexual identification in which the son is in love with his mother and the daughter with her father. In this unconscious dynamic a girl first connects with her own sexuality, her own deep femininity, through her relationship with her father. Later this projection is broken when the girl falls in love with another man, but it can often be complicated by the daughter's being her father's anima figure, "Daddy's little girl," whom he does not want to lose to another man.[30] But the dreamer's father has given her a ring made of four silver threads. Silver is the color of the feminine, and four the number of psychological wholeness. This ring symbolizes her feminine wholeness, which was given her by this first relationship.

For our dreamer, the king, who symbolizes collective masculine values, in particular the goals of material wealth, became identified with her father, and as his mistress she was never true to herself. She was governed by what she felt she ought to be, rather than experiencing her true nature. Even in consciously rebelling against her father's values she was still unconsciously a slave to them; she was still his mistress. But the dynamics of the psyche do not follow the laws of reason. Jung said of the path of individuation that "the longest way is often the shortest." The king, her father, gave her something most precious: her own complete femininity.

Although the ring is a symbol of her own femininity, the fact that the four silver strands are twisted suggests that, in her relationship with her king and father, her feminine self had become twisted. She had not been true to herself and so twisted the strands of her real nature. Now that she stands naked and is no longer the king's mistress, she is able to "untwist the four strands of silver wire," under which is something infinitely precious, a "fine, gold filament." This gold hair is a gift from the Beloved, given long, long ago:

> Before there was a trace of this world of men,
> I carried the memory of a lock of your hair,
> A stray end gathered within me, though unknown....
>
> From the moment of time's first drawn breath,
> Love resides in us,
> A treasure locked into the heart's hidden vault.[31]

This image of the fine gold hair is the same love-token as in the dream of the gift of a box in which there was a single hair. However deep it is hidden, we all carry this love-token within our hearts. It is the golden thread that will take us home. The way home is a lover's return into the arms of the Beloved; to make that journey we must follow the thread of love that we have within us. Sometimes we don't find this thread; we search all over the world but never look "into the heart's hidden vault." Sometimes, as with the dreamer, we hardly notice it, because it is "dull from being hidden so long." But it is always there, waiting to be found. St. Gregory of Nyssa wrote that "The path of Love is like a bridge of hair across a chasm of fire," and the dreamer recognizes that the golden hair is that bridge. With this recognition her heart opens and she is filled with an "overwhelming, indescribable feeling of love."

Love is the greatest power in creation. It is the energy that transforms the seeker, dissolving the veils of separation. "All you need is love," for this power of the heart will take us where we cannot even imagine. The heart is as big as the universe; everything is contained within it. In the words of the Prophet, "My earth and My heaven containeth Me not, but the heart of My faithful servant containeth Me."[32]

Our dreamer has found the talisman of her real Beloved and is "magically transported" to the prince's bedchamber. They are to be married and he will then be the new king. The mystic marriage is a sacred commitment in which everything is surrendered into the hands of love. The values of the old king have gone and all that remains is the look from the Beloved's eyes, the tender touch of His hands. Her prince is waiting for her to join Him, as He has been waiting for aeons. Within the heart He is always waiting, nearer to us than we know:

> *And He is with you*
> with you
> in your search
> when you seek Him
> look for Him
> in your looking
> closer to you
> than yourself
> to yourself.[33]

Our dreamer has found Him, found the place where He has been waiting, the bed where He will embrace her. She feels the presence of her prince but does not see his face, for he is in truth an invisible lover. He is without form, just as love itself is without form.

Her love for her prince will take her home. He will become everything for her and their love will transform her. When she wakes from the dream she knows this; she knows that she is going home. But then she is "overtaken with tremendous grief, longing, and the feeling of painful separation." One sip of the wine of love and one is lost forever. The world turns sour and one will do anything, even die, for just another sip. In the words of Abû Sa'îd ibn Abî-l-Khayr, "Love is God's trap," and the pain of separation is a poison that slowly kills us, until we no longer exist, and all that remains is the Beloved.

THE FEMININE SIDE OF LOVE

The source of my grief and loneliness is deep in my breast.
This is a disease no doctor can cure.
Only union with the Friend can cure it.

Râbi'a[1]

The Pain of Love

Everything in the universe has a dual nature: positive and negative, masculine and feminine. The masculine side of love is "I love you." Love's feminine quality is "I am waiting for you; I am longing for you." For the Sufi it is the feminine side of love—the longing, the cup waiting to be filled—that takes the seeker home into the arms of the Beloved. The lover knows that longing is the most precious poison, as is expressed in a Sufi's prayer:

> Give me the pain of Love, the Pain of Love
> for Thee!
> Not the joy of Love, just the Pain of Love,
> And I will pay the price, any price you
> ask!
> All myself I offer for it, and the price
> you will ask on top of it!
> Keep the joy for others, give me the Pain,
> And gladly I will pay for the Pain of Love![2]

This longing, this pain in the heart, is planted like a seed by the One who knocks on the door of our heart and calls us to Him. Before we look for Him, He must first look upon us. Then, when He wants us for Himself, He poisons us with longing. This poison brings about a painful death, as we die to the world of the ego. Sometimes it begins with a sense of discontent, what Saint Thomas Aquinas called "the divine discontent." Nothing in life seems quite right; something is missing but one does not know what. There is a dull ache in the unconscious that begins to force itself upon our attention. Slowly the outer world loses its attraction, and it begins to dawn upon our consciousness that we want something else, something that does not belong to this world. Then the spiritual search begins. We meditate, aspire, look for a teacher, and as we do, so the ache in the heart begins to burn, the longing to grow. The more we aspire, the more we blow upon the flames in the heart. The tears that we cry are the homesickness of the soul and these tears point out the path. The pain of love has only one cure: "Only union with the Friend can cure it." Not only is it our pain, but because He is not other than us, it is also the pain of His love for us. It takes us along the burning road that leads to the death of the ego. He will not allow any other comfort than His touch, any other healing than His embrace. A story from the life of the ninth-century Sufi, Dhû-l-Nûn, the Egyptian, illustrates this:

> I was wandering in the mountains when I observed a party of afflicted folk gathered together.
>
> "What befell you?" I asked.
>
> "There is a devotee living in a cell here," they answered. "Once every year he comes out and

> breathes on these people and they are all healed. Then he returns to his cell, and does not emerge again until the following year."
>
> I waited patiently until he came out. I beheld a man pale of cheek, wasted and with sunken eyes. The awe of him caused me to tremble. He looked on the multitude with compassion. Then he raised his eyes to heaven, and breathed several times over the afflicted ones. All were healed.
>
> As he was about to retire to his cell, I seized his skirt. "For the love of God," I cried. "You have healed the outward sickness; pray heal the inward sickness."
>
> "Dhû-l-Nûn," he said, gazing at me, "take your hand from me. The Friend is watching from the zenith of might and majesty. If He sees you clutching at another than He, He will abandon you to that person, and that person to you, and you will perish each at the other's hand."
>
> So saying, he withdrew into his cell.[3]

Sometimes we try to run away from this pain, hide ourselves in other corners of our life. In the complexities of the mind and its barrage of doubts we can try to deny this call:

> I fled Him, down the nights and down the
> days;
> I fled Him, down the arches of the years:
> I fled Him, down the labyrinthine ways
> Of my own mind; and in the midst of tears
> I hid from Him, and under running laughter.[4]

But once the Great Lover has looked into our heart and planted His longing there, however far we flee from Him we carry within us our own deepest secret: that He wants us for Himself. Still we try to hide from Him because we know in our heart what it means, we know the price we must pay; we know the loneliness and the pain. Longing brings into our minds every doubt and every fear. Are we prepared to give up everything, even ourselves, for something of which the mind knows nothing? Do we want the beyond of the beyond? A woman had the following dream soon after she first came to our group:

> The teacher stood in front of me and said, "You should wear your hair back like this and have a white cashmere sweater." But I replied, "No. I want the beyond of the beyond." Then the teacher grew in size and became enormous, vast and threatening, and said, "Is this what you really want?" And I said, "Yes." Then the teacher became smaller and said, "Actually it won't be too difficult."

This dreamer had suffered much in her life and her inner discontent had isolated her for many years before she came to our group. She had been pushed to the point where she knew what she wanted and was prepared to pay the price, which was to face her deepest fears and her own inner pain. If we surrender to the process and accept the suffering which His imprint will bring, then we allow Him to carry us home. If we resist, He will take us to Him anyway, for as much as we may fight, He is stronger. But the quickest road is to let go. In the following dream another friend "missed an opportunity" because he did not let go and allow himself to be killed:

> A carousel is going round and round and I am holding on. The centrifugal force is such that it can easily break my neck but I tense my neck muscles. I am told that I have missed an opportunity.

This dreamer was not yet ready to pay the ultimate price, himself. Other opportunities would follow, but he would have to learn how to give himself away, how to allow himself to be taken.

Surrendering to the Path

On the Sufi path the greatest importance is given to surrender. We have to learn to surrender to the inner alchemy that will transform us. The seeker does nothing; he simply allows this process to take place. It is a process that takes us far beyond the ego. It can never be grasped by the mind, for it belongs to the mystery of the heart. The veils of separation cannot be removed by the wayfarer, only by the Beloved:

> Know that you are your own veil which conceals yourself from you. Know also that you cannot reach God through yourself, but that you reach Him through Him. The reason is that when He vouchsafes the vision of reaching Him, He calls upon you to seek after Him and you do so.[5]

He calls us and we follow the call, allowing ourselves to be led, blindfold, back into the core of our being. This is a circular journey in which we are spun so fast we lose all sense of direction. In the following dream it begins with the dreamer's longing:

> I am in a community and people are going about their business, but I feel a longing inside me and go out onto an open plain. I feel this longing and pray for a sign. Then on the horizon I see a little white cloud. It starts to grow very rapidly and becomes gold-vermilion. It comes above me and golden light starts to fall. I am sucked into this cloud and spun around very fast. It is a tremendous experience, after which I feel very thin and weak, but my husband comes and holds me in his arms. Then a young girl comes and asks me to help her have this experience, but I just point at her heart and say, "It's all in there. I can't do anything; you have to do it yourself."

This dream starts with the dreamer in the ordinary, everyday world, with people "going about their business." But the dreamer feels a longing inside her and so she leaves the community and goes "out onto an open plain." At the beginning of the path our inner longing turns us away from the everyday world and the hustle and bustle of life. Later, this same path will lead the wayfarer back into the marketplace to take part in the everyday affairs of life, with the difference that she will be in the world but not of the world. This is the Sufi practice of "solitude in the crowd": whatever one's outward activity, the inner attention remains in the heart; in each moment of the day there is continual remembrance, as expressed by Abû Sa'îd ibn Abî-l-Khayr:

> The perfect mystic is not an ecstatic devotee lost in contemplation of Oneness, nor a saintly recluse shunning all commerce with mankind, but "the true saint" goes in and out amongst the people and eats and sleeps with them and buys and sells in the market and marries and takes part in social intercourse, and never forgets God for a single moment.[6]

The Process of Introversion

In order to reach this state of inner detachment there needs to be a period of withdrawal, a process of turning one's attention away from the outer world and reconnecting with the inner core of one's being. This process of withdrawal does not mean that the wayfarer physically retires into seclusion, but rather that there is a period of introversion, a descent into the depths of the unconscious in order to find one's true foundation, the rock of the Self. This period of introversion is often lonely and involves breaking the old patterns in which external life was lived from the perspective of the ego and patterns of conditioning. The alchemists called this stage the *putrefactio*. Putrefaction is the rotting that breaks down dead bodies. The old structures of consciousness have to be broken down before the new can be born.

This stage of introspection also has the quality of "brooding," as the energy of consciousness withdraws into the unconscious. To quote Carl Jung:

> The attention given to the unconscious has the effect of incubation, a brooding over the slow fire needed in the initial stages of the work.... It is really as if attention warmed the unconscious and activated it, thereby breaking down the barriers that separated it from consciousness.[7]

The energy which is withdrawn into the unconscious is needed to hatch the egg, the symbol of potential wholeness and new birth. This wholeness will be the Self, the union of consciousness and the unconscious, which is also a preexistent center of consciousness. As an egg it has always existed in the depths of the psyche, but it needs this inner concentration of energy in order to be hatched and become conscious. After a period of depression another friend had the following dream, which points to the coming into consciousness of an aspect of her real nature. The dream made her feel happy for days:

> There was a white flower made up of tiny white flowers, and in these flowers there were eggs. One eggshell broke and inside there was a boy clothed in white. There was the most beautiful feeling about this, and a voice said, "This time the birth will not be difficult."

The awakening of the Self is the most natural process; it is the natural flowering of the soul. But like all natural processes it needs to be tended with care and attention. One must learn to listen within and pay attention to the needs of the psyche, and not judge by outer values. A seeming depression may be an important period of "brooding."

This stage of the inner work usually requires much of the wayfarer's attention and psychic energy. Therefore during this period there is very little excess energy that can be put into one's external life, which may appear to be undergoing a time of stagnation. Similarly the wayfarer is often advised not to attempt any new or demanding life project, but to live as simple and undemanding a life as possible. The whole structure of the psyche is being altered and maximum inner attention must be given to this work. One friend who had deep counseling and healing skills spent this time doing the most mundane job as receptionist in a garage. Each time she tried to change this job for something more interesting, she was given a hint to remain.

It is very important that this process of inner readjustment be completed before the outer world begins to make extra demands. Otherwise when external pressure is applied the individual will revert to previous patterns and conditioned responses, and the work that has been done in centering on the Self is rendered useless. One needs to develop the quality of patience that allows the inner processes to mature in their own time, and to hold the space in the psyche so that the desires of the ego or the attitudes of a masculine, goal-oriented culture do not interfere. Moreover, because such "feminine" soul-work is alien to our culture, it often requires great strength and courage not to interfere with it. In the words of Lao Tsu:

> Do you have the patience to wait
> till your mud settles and the water is clear?
> Can you remain unmoving
> till the right action arises by itself?[8]

This "work without doing" is our natural way of being, but like many aspects of the feminine, it has been repressed and forgotten. The Sufi path teaches us to trust and surrender to something deeper than the ego, to develop the feminine qualities of waiting and patience. Thus we are able to remember the wisdom of our own natural unfolding and the natural harmony in which the inner and outer work together. When the inner processes are complete, the outer situation will often change of its own accord. When it was time for this friend's inner potential as a therapist and healer to be fully used in service to others, the job as a garage receptionist ended by itself.

The fact that we live in a culture that does not value inner work has created a negative collective conditioning that is encountered by anyone who turns away from the outer world to look within. This collective pressure makes us doubt the importance of what we are doing. Old friends will question us, may even attack our need to look within. In abandoning the ego-goals of the external world, we are confronting a powerful collective force, a conditioning that is itself threatened by anyone who sincerely seeks to find something deeper. Furthermore, because the urge to turn away from the world does not come from the ego, but from deep within the unconscious, the conscious mind does not understand what is happening and is therefore easily influenced by collective pressure. This is why a spiritual group is so important. A group of sincere seekers provides a sacred space which values the inner processes and to some degree protects the aspirant from the collective forces that try to undermine inner work. This is one of the reasons that the Sufis give so much significance to just being together. Meditating, sharing dreams, or just talking about everyday things, wayfarers support each other, create a home away from home in which spiritual aspirations are not attacked but accepted and understood.

The Sufi group provides great support, but on the path there is always the danger that any support can become a limitation, an obstacle to the wayfarer's standing on her own feet, making her own individual journey. There is always the danger that introversion can become stagnation, that withdrawal can become escapism. If there is the danger of this happening, the teacher will follow the ancient tradition of throwing the seeker out of the group. Irina Tweedie spent a year and a half with her Sufi teacher, Bhai Sahib, before he sent her back to England, sending her off with anger, in order to force her to experience a complete outer break with him: "Go!... I don't want to see your ugly face again! Go away!" Thrown out, one is thrown upon oneself, for although the Sufi group is a refuge when it is needed, it is never allowed to limit the development of the seeker. It is a place for creative work, not for escape.

The Paradox of the Effortless Path

In the dream in which the dreamer's longing took her away from people, out onto the open plain, the process of introversion and turning away from the world was just beginning. But the dream outlined the course of her inner journey, helped her to understand what would happen. Dreams are signposts, and at important moments in our life they often point out the path we are to follow, so that we can consciously cooperate with the changes that are happening in both our inner and outer lives.

On the open plain the dreamer prays for a sign, for an answer to her longing. When the longing starts to burn within the heart we cry from the very depths, and such a cry is always answered, though sometimes it is answered in a way that we cannot see or understand. For this dreamer the answer is a little white cloud appearing on the horizon. A cloud symbolizes a message from God, which here appears on the horizon of her consciousness and then comes towards her, growing and becoming gold-vermilion. The dreamer had recently come to our Sufi group, which belongs to the Naqshbandi tradition. Naqshbandis are known as the "silent Sufis" because they practice the silent *dhikr*, the silent repetition of the name of God; they are also known as the "Golden Sufis," because the color of the energy of this path is golden yellow. The energy of this path had come into her life, was now being lived with the bright red vermilion of life. This energy was an answer to the prayer she had cried in her desolation and aloneness. In the dream it comes above her as a cloud and "golden light" falls like rain. The grace of God falls like rain and is His gift to those who have turned their faces away from the world to seek Him.

The dreamer is then "sucked into this cloud and spun around very fast." She is taken into the energy of the path which will transform her totally. In this Naqshbandi Sufi system we are spun so fast we lose all sense of direction and in the end we lose everything; everything is thrown off by the spinning. The energy of the path activates the heart *chakra,* spinning it faster and faster. This increases the energy of love which is the driving force of spiritual transformation. It is an effortless path because everything is given. The disciple does nothing but allow this energy to transform her, to allow everything to be taken away. In a dream mentioned earlier, the dreamer resisted this energy, tensed his neck and did not let it be broken, and so was told that he had "missed an opportunity." Here the dreamer lets herself be sucked in and spun around. It is "a tremendous experience."

After this tremendous experience the dreamer feels thin and weak. This echoes a dream Irina Tweedie had in which she was looking at herself in a mirror and saw that she was very thin and pale. Her teacher, Bhai Sahib, gave her this interpretation: "It is a very good dream. Thin and thinner, until nothing will remain."[9] Everything must go—all attachments, all desires. In order to realize the Eternal Nothingness, the Reality of Realities, the ego must die; we must become nothing.

The dreamer's being "thin and weak" also reflects the fact that the spiritual energies that produce this transformation are very powerful. Their intensity is often bewildering, and the process of inner change can be very exhausting, both physically and psychologically. In particular, these energies work on the sympathetic and parasympathetic nervous systems. These are the autonomic nervous systems that function below the threshold of consciousness. According to Jung, "the unconscious is largely identical with the sympathetic and parasympathetic systems, which are the physiological counterparts of the polarity of unconscious contents."[10] The spiritual energies, working on these nervous systems, activate the contents of the unconscious. Therefore, on the physical level it is important to take care of the physical body by exercising and eating well, and also to be prepared for emotional stress, as all the repressed feelings and past pain come to the surface and are cleared out. Although it is an effortless path because everything is given, great effort is required to hold on in spite of everything, to allow this painful and totally demanding inner process to take place.

When the dreamer feels thin and weak, her husband "comes and holds me in his arms." He represents her animus, the masculine aspect of a woman's psyche, which provides her with the inner strength necessary to contain the processes of transformation. The animus is the figure which mediates between the inner world of the feminine and the external world; thus his positive support will enable her to integrate her inner experiences into the fabric of everyday life.

In the final image of the dream a young girl comes and asks the dreamer to help her have this experience. But the dreamer just points at her heart and says "It's all in there. I can't do anything; you have to do it yourself." This response points to the paradox of the effortless path: although everything is given, you have to do it all yourself. A man once came to our group and asked someone about what the teacher did. "Does she teach you?" "No," was the reply. "Does she give practices?" Again the answer was "No." "What does she do then?" "Nothing; you have to do it all yourself." The man left and never returned.

The Naqshbandi Sufi path, as I have experienced it, has little outward form or structure. At our meetings we meditate, drink tea, and discuss dreams. Within the dynamic of the group the individual is given the opportunity to work upon himself, to meditate, aspire, to go deep within the unconscious and accept both the light and the darkness that are found there. The path to the beyond is unique for each seeker. There are as many ways to God as there are human beings, and this journey demands that we each make the ultimate effort. To follow the thread that is hidden in the heart is the most demanding task life can offer. And the teacher can only point out the way; even the great teachers like Christ, Muhammad, and Buddha could do no more than this. Buddha's last words to Ananda speak this spiritual truth:

> Therefore, O Ananda, take thyself for a light, take thyself for a refuge. Do not seek for a refuge in anything else. Work on thy salvation diligently.

Every effort is required to walk along a path that is as narrow as the edge of a sword. Two cannot walk together, for it is the journey of the soul back to the Source, an offering of our own unique self back to the Creator. Within the group the seeker is given immense support, but there comes the time when any external support becomes a limitation, and one must continue alone. Even in the midst of family life and surrounded by loving friends, one finds oneself so deeply alone that it is like being in an empty desert with only the sound of the wind howling. Such inner states totally overshadow external circumstances. This stage on the effortless path was beautifully imaged in a dream in which people were sliding down a golden slide, but there came a point where the slide narrowed and everyone had to go through alone. It is only when we are totally alone that we find Him in our hearts. It is such an intimate relationship that there is no space for anything else.

From a spiritual perspective we are never alone; we are looked after more than we could ever know. The moment we turn towards Him, He takes us in His arms and provides us with everything we need. The spiritual journey requires every effort, and yet is effortless. We slide home to the Beloved but we pay with the blood of the heart. "How can there be effort with Divine things? They are GIVEN."[11] But to receive them, to make our cup empty and offer it into His Emptiness, takes every effort. Abû Sa'îd al-Kharrâz summed up this paradox:

> Whoever believes he can reach God by his own efforts toils in vain; whoever believes he can reach God without effort is merely a traveller on the road of intent.[12]

A Natural State of Being

There are two ways to attract God's love: either we become perfect, and He has to love us; or we offer our whole self to Him in utter humility, and He cannot help but love us. The Sufi chooses the latter path, that of the lover who waits for the Beloved. The following two dreams point to differences between the masculine and the feminine attitudes to spiritual life. They were dreamt by a man. The first dream he had before he came to our group, the second dream after he had spent an afternoon sitting with us.

> FIRST DREAM: I am driving very fast up a road which goes into the sky. I am driving into the sun and cannot see. The road curves to the right but I go straight on.
>
> SECOND DREAM: Beside me sits an American Indian in *dhyana* meditation. The sun in the sky is coming towards us.

The first dream images a masculine, goal-oriented approach to spiritual life. The dreamer is driving as fast as he can into the sun. The spiritual quest is always a journey into the unknown, and the dreamer cannot see where he is going; but, even when the road curves to the right, he goes "straight on." The attitude in the second dream is very different; it is imaged by an American Indian sitting in *dhyana*. *Dhyana* is the meditation of the heart practiced on this Sufi path. The wayfarer fills the heart with love, and as thoughts come into the mind, they are drowned in the heart. Technically it is not meditation, but a form of yogic relaxation, in which, as the heart *chakra* is activated, the individual mind is thrown into the universal mind. Through surrendering the mind to the heart, the seeker surrenders the ego to the energies of love that will transform the psyche and give birth to the Self. Rather than the dreamer's driving into the sun, which is a symbol of the Self, "the sun in the sky is coming towards us."

The figure of the American Indian points towards the feminine nature of this path, which works in harmony with the deepest forces of nature. Traditionally, the American Indians lived in harmony with nature and saw everything as part of one sacred whole. They understood the natural rhythms of life and their spiritual purposes. Just as the Indians saw the outer workings of nature as symbolic and sacred, so can we see her inner workings as holy, and learn to live in harmony with our inner nature and the instinctual energy that flows deep within the psyche. The forces of the unconscious transform us and make us whole, for the Golden Flower of the Self is "an image born of nature's own working, a natural symbol far removed from all conscious intention."[13]

On the pathless path there is nowhere to go. Everything must be given up; even the idea of a goal is a limitation. A friend had the following dream just before he died:

> I'm with some people thinking of "the goal" and I get the idea that I have no goal and I give it up and let go of it. There follows a peacefulness, joy, and truthfulness not to be put into words. The teacher comes and hugs me around my belly. I carry this wonderful state wherever I go. I know it is a natural state not to have a goal.

The Self is a state of being. It is our natural state, and yet we can never reach it on our own. We can never find it unless we are shown. We must make every effort and yet it is given as a gift. To quote Abû'l-Hasan Kharaqânî:

> Whoever states that he has attained God, has not, whereas whoever states that he has been taken to God, has indeed attained union with God.

To know oneself is to know God. To be totally oneself is to be totally God. There is no difference, there is no duality. This is the experience of merging, when He merges into His lover. This state can never be described, but it can be hinted at. The man who had the previous dream about letting go of the goal also had the following dream which was an experience of realizing the Self:

I dreamed I was totally me. God dwells in me as me. I dreamed that I got up and wrote it all down. It was so beautiful, so precise, wonderful. I don't have time to think about the future! God in me makes me perfect. I need nothing. I had thought I wrote it all down and finally realized I hadn't. Can I recapture it? Of course! It's me—it's God—so terribly, shamelessly me. Beyond sexual intimacy—supreme. Just lowly me, and lowly me is all-powerful, but can't be bothered with power. Power over what? There's nothing to have power over. It's not ecstasy in the old sense. I mean there's no object-subject—just perfect me, God as little me, inviolable, inexpressible. I seemed (in the dream) to have all the words, but I hadn't written it down. No matter! I affirm it anyway.

Listen, there's no Teacher or any other form in this. I'm all alone. There's no group—there doesn't have to be. Anybody in the group who experiences this knows he needs nobody else. I am all of them when I am absolutely, lovingly myself.

All along I've been this—just didn't let it happen. Just as Bhai Sahib said, "The Beloved merges with me, *not* the other way around." What a difference that makes!

THE ALCHEMICAL OPUS I: THE TRANSFORMATION OF THE SHADOW

One does not become enlightened by imagining figures of light, but by making the darkness conscious. The latter procedure, however, is disagreeable and therefore not popular.

C. G. Jung[1]

Descent into Darkness

On the Sufi path the energy of love transforms the seeker. The pain of longing purifies us, burning away the veils of separation. But this love is no idealized romance, but rather a passionate affair of the soul that takes us deep within, confronting us with our own darkness. Soon after a woman came to our Sufi group she had the following dream:

> I am being kissed by a man. It is the most wonderful experience. It is not sexual, just a pure feeling of love in the heart. It touches me very deeply. But then I feel a tongue in my mouth, and it is not his tongue. I open my eyes and see that I am embracing a serpent, and it is the serpent's tongue in my mouth. I feel very frightened.

This dream begins with the love affair that is the essence of the path, the relationship of lover and

Beloved. But then the lover turns into a serpent, symbolizing the deepest, most primordial levels of the psyche. Love draws us into this darkness, into the hidden places of our own being. The wayfarer is confronted with all that has been rejected, unacknowledged, and repressed. Irina Tweedie describes how this most challenging work was very different from what she expected when she met her Sufi teacher:

> I had hoped for instructions in Yoga, expected wonderful teachings, but what the Teacher did was mainly to force me to face the darkness within myself, and it almost killed me. In other words he made me "descend into hell," the cosmic drama enacted in every soul as soon as it dares lift its face to the Light.[2]

The energy of love activates the unconscious, bringing us face to face with our own darkness, enabling us to purify the psyche and prepare a space where lover and Beloved can meet.

The Birth of the Shadow

Only when the sun is directly above do we not cast a shadow; only in the full light of the Self do we not have a dark side. Otherwise our own darkness, although hidden, is always present, peering from the shadows of the unconscious. Chasing us down dark alleyways, hammering on the doors of our dreams, our shadow comes to meet us.

We long to stay in the light and keep our darkness hidden, to look towards the heavens and deny the tortuous corridors of our inner self. But all inner work begins with work upon the shadow. It is the basic foundation of any psychological or spiritual path. One friend had an auspicious first day at our group. The toilet drains had become blocked, and he offered to help clear them. Rather than sitting in meditation, he spent his first afternoon standing in sewage and unblocking the pipes. When the teacher heard about this she said that it was a very auspicious sign: it showed that he meant business. For the next few years he worked psychologically on what he had begun symbolically. He went into the world of the shadow and cleaned out his own mess.

But what is this shadow, this inner darkness? Where did it come from? Why does it haunt us? The shadow belongs to the world of duality, to the world in which light and darkness oppose each other. In the primal oneness of the Self there is no shadow; in the dazzling darkness of the beyond there is no differentiation between light and darkness. As a child we come into this world from oneness, and in the eyes of a baby one can still glimpse an undivided wholeness. But as we take on the clothes of this world, so we become caught in its play of duality. The child's first experience of this duality is often in his experience of the good and bad breast. In different ways duality begins to break up our inner experience of wholeness, and we are gradually expelled from paradise.

Mankind, with the gift of consciousness, has the ability to know good and evil, to accept and to reject, to differentiate good from bad, to turn away from the darkness and look to the light. The price of the evolution of consciousness is the shadow, because what has been rejected, what has been labeled "bad," does not disappear, but constellates in the unconscious where it takes on a life of its own. Thus the shadow is born, the psychological split between the ego and its dark twin.

Our consciousness creates our shadow, and as we grow up and take on the clothing and values of our culture, we begin to be weighed down by this rejected self. The wayfarer who wishes to make the journey home has to confront the split within himself, has to descend into his inner darkness and undertake the psychological work of confronting and integrating the shadow. He has to accept his own dark side, what Jung describes as

> the "negative" side of the personality, the sum of all those unpleasant qualities we like to hide, together with the insufficiently developed functions and contents of the personal unconscious.[3]

Consciousness creates the shadow, but the character of our dark twin is usually determined by our family and culture. In *A Little Book on the Human Shadow* Robert Bly suggests that when we were one or two years old we were a whole ball of energy until we began to notice "that our parents didn't like certain parts of that ball."[4] In order to be loved and accepted, the child begins to put parts of itself into an invisible bag that is carried behind. We are told not to be angry and so anger goes into the bag. If certain feelings are not allowed to be expressed in the family, even feelings of love and tenderness, they find their way into this invisible bag, which slowly grows full of one's own energy, energy that has no place in the external world. Alice Miller, in *The Drama of the Gifted Child*, describes how the more intelligent, the more "gifted," the child, the more completely he or she will adapt to what the external world values. Love and affection are "bought" by filling the bag with one's own precious individuality, which by its very nature often makes unwelcome demands.

Then, as we grow up and go to school, different sets of pressures come to bear that force parts of ourselves out of the sunlight and into the darkness. Competition, the drive to work hard, and most of all the peer pressure to fit in can result in more of our own true self's being discarded to fester in the murky corners of our lives, in our moods and reactions.

In the journey towards adulthood we become individuals and develop conscious identities. But at the same time the opposite—that which we have no wish to be—constellates in the darkness. The ego develops its dark twin, and often the stronger the ego the darker the shadow; the greater the strength of the conscious self, the more power it has to repress unwanted aspects into the unconscious. If one is brought up to be independent and value self-sufficiency, a needy child will then begin to cry in the darkness. The greater the drive towards independence, the louder are the unheard cries of the child. The unacknowledged desire to be mothered and looked after can easily harden into coldness, a coldness towards one's own vulnerability and needs, towards the child one carries within. The child then appears through projection: those people who express their own neediness evoke anger or disgust—"Why can't they look after themselves? Why are they so needy, so wanting to be mothered?"

Caught in the duality of our shadow, we project its darkness onto others. We dislike or find unbearable a sibling, a classmate, or neighbor, not realizing that it is our own rejected self to which we are reacting. The power of projection is that we do not need to acknowledge our own faults, to look our darkness in the face. But for some people there comes the time when so much energy and unlived potential are caught in this dynamic of projection, so much of our inner self is trapped through rejection, that we feel the need to reclaim our shadow. Then, if we follow our negative reactions to others, they will lead us to this rejected self:

> I looked and looked, and saw and saw
> That what I thought was you and you
> Is really me and me.

First we have to find the shadow. Then once it is acknowledged, it can be embraced. To acknowledge the shadow does not mean to live it out; we do not have to become a needy child. Rather we have to accept our shadow, nurture the child from within. If our shadow is bitchiness or cruelty, we have to look at and love that despised part of ourself. Such confrontation is no easy task: it is always easier to blame someone else. Moreover, as we start to acknowledge our own faults and inadequacies, the ego identity which we have so carefully constructed begins to crumble:

> The individual's specious unity that emphatically says "I want, I think" breaks down under the impact of the unconscious. So long as [the individual] can think that somebody else (his father or mother) is responsible for his difficulties, he can save some semblance of unity.... But once he realizes that he himself has a shadow, that his enemy is in his own heart, then the conflict begins and one becomes two.[5]

An awareness of the opposites in one's own nature at first brings conflict between the ego and the shadow, and the individual is thrown, often violently, between the two. This is a very painful process, for one loses any stable identity, and instead experiences an inner battlefield as opposing aspects of oneself fight it out. On this battlefield previously unacknowledged parts of oneself demand to be recognized, demand "a place in the sun."

Seeking a greater wholeness, seeking to reconcile the opposites within us, we find ourself caught in conflicts that are painful and bitter. Outer arguments pale beside the inner struggles that can be violent and tormenting. Christ's paradoxical statement clearly defines the battle of opposites, and yet also reminds us that this battle is for a higher purpose:

> Think not that I am come to send peace on earth:
> I came not to send peace, but a sword.
> For I am to set a man at variance against his father, and the daughter against her mother, and the daughter in law against her mother in law.[6]

The light and power of the Self, for which Christ is a symbol, dynamically constellate the opposites and throw us into their conflict. Our own psyche becomes a battleground for the work of transformation. The higher energies of our own being break us apart before the deeper work of integration can take place. We cannot enter the sacred space of our own inner being before this preliminary work is done.

But not only do we experience the inner conflict of ego and shadow, we also feel the pain of what has been rejected and repressed. The energy of the shadow which now comes into consciousness often carries with it pain and vulnerability, suffering and sadness. Moreover, in the dark confines of the shadow, psychic energy cannot flow freely, and just as stagnant water becomes polluted, so too does the discarded life energy. In the dark, locked rooms of the unconscious no healing can occur, only deepening despair, anger, and resentment. Then, just as a rejected and abused child can only respond with anger or pain, so do the contents of our shadow become resentful. When we open the door to the unconscious, we should be prepared for these painful and difficult feelings to surface.

But the shadow is not necessarily negative, for it can contain unrealized potential and creativity. In the Western world we have become so "civilized" that our instinctual self is often the shadow. Then we live out of harmony with our own natural rhythm, and our own vitality is locked in the darkness, often personified by a primitive person or, to a white person, a black man or woman. Our imaginative nature has also only too often been repressed into the darkness, and in particular there is little place for it in our intellectually oriented education. Children live naturally in their imaginative worlds, but when they go to school they are encouraged to think linearly and told to stop dreaming. So the imagination is easily discarded, and television takes the place of creative fantasies. Repressed, our imaginative self comes to us only in dreams, when our conscious mind is asleep. Or, expressing itself through the shadow, it may reappear as grotesque fantasies or even as physical pain—if that is the only way for it to gain attention. To mistreat one's inner imaginative self and neglect its transformative energy can result in that energy's being misplaced.

Then a rejected dream figure, an abused serpent, for example, becomes a backache that can be so powerful we have to stay in bed. In previous ages the medicine man listened to the interplay of the inner and outer, the symbolic and the physical; we are only now beginning to reawaken to this wisdom. The inner world is more powerful than we have been conditioned to believe.

Unto the Third and Fourth Generation

The spiritual path takes us into the unconscious where we encounter our own shadow, our rejected, unloved self. In these murky waters we will meet not only our personal darkness, but also our dark family heritage. Every family has its skeletons, which are kept carefully locked away from consciousness, and they are often powerful bonding agents holding a family together with shared guilt or co-dependency. This bond of darkness can last for generations, as expressed in the saying "the sins of the fathers shall be visited upon the children unto the third and fourth generation."

In this shared darkness individual members of the family may also carry the shadow of others. In particular children carry the shadow of their parents, which is one of the reasons that the relationship between grandparents and grandchildren lacks the conflicts that dominate many parent-child relationships.

A child grows up in the psychic atmosphere of his parents. The repressed shadow of the parents dominates this psychic soup, and the child easily "picks it up." Also the parent can unknowingly project his or her shadow onto a child. For example, my father came from a background in which a man could never express his feelings, where the English idea of the "stiff upper lip" prevailed. He deeply loved his mother who died when I was two years old. There was no place for his feelings, which expressed the more vulnerable, feminine side of his nature. It was thirty years later, after his death, that I discovered that these repressed feelings had become implanted in my psyche. From the age of two I had carried the sensitivity and vulnerability of his feminine self.

From generation to generation such patterns can be passed on in the unconscious. Only when they are consciously accepted is the chain broken, and then not only the future but also the past is healed. One friend inherited a family shadow which involved always trying to prove that he was not a failure. He was driven by the need to succeed, but so strong was the failure pattern that just as success seemed imminent something "went wrong," and the business plan, the new project, failed. For a long time he experienced a mounting despair as he realized that he was caught in a pattern which it was beyond his power to break. But finally freedom came not through his being a success, but by his being able to observe this pattern, to watch how it unfolded in both his father's life and his own. Consciousness is a powerful force against the psychological patterns which imprison us. Its light enters the dark world of the shadow and transforms it. We have become so conditioned to value only actions that we have forgotten the power of being and watching. Through watching (*muraqaba* in Sufi terminology), by observing the dynamic of his family pattern, this friend freed himself from the compulsive drive that dragged him towards success and inevitably into failure. He also lifted the curse from the shoulders of his father. He untied a web that had been woven over the decades.

We carry the weight of both our personal shadow and a family shadow, as well as the deeper, collective shadow of our culture. The phrase "black sheep of the family" reflects the fact that it is often on the shoulders of one person that the family shadow rests most heavily. Because of the way the unconscious forces work, it is usually the most sensitive member of the family who carries the shadow. Being sensitive, the "black sheep" is most easily susceptible to the collective pressure, and unconsciously takes on the dark family secret. On a deeper level he or she may also carry the responsibility of turning round and looking the family shadow in the face, and so transforming it. It is the one cast out from the tents who can often bring healing.

The Stone Which the Builders Refused

The shadow has the dual dynamic of darkness and redemption. It carries our wholeness; it is the dark twin that leads to our completion. Only through the acceptance of our shadow do we discover our essential nature, "the face we had before we were born." There is another secret to the shadow which was understood by the ancient alchemists: working on one's shadow takes one into the depths of the inner world, and it is there that the light of the Self is to be found. This is the "light hidden in darkness," the king's son who "lies in the dark depths of the sea as though dead, but yet lives and calls from the deep: 'Whosoever will free me from the waters and lead me to dry land, him will I prosper with everlasting riches.'"[7] One of the mysteries of the psychological process is that only through our fully experiencing and accepting the inner darkness is the inner light revealed; only then does the transformation occur. This whole process is outlined in the following dream:

> There was a basement which led downstairs to a locked door. There was a feeling of great danger there. I didn't want to go in but I knew that someday I had to. As I was leaving, a huge ferocious beast with great teeth came after me. I ran away and it charged after me. Then it came in another form, as a grey Volvo car with huge grates on the front. It pulled up and this woman got out. She was emanating cruelty. I knew that she was very dangerous, but she was in a form that was safe. Then at the end of the dream I am watching a parade and there is a beautiful green star with golden letters which spell "ALCHEMY."

Behind the locked door in the basement lives the shadow. Repressed into the unconscious, our rejected self is often locked away, and then, like a caged beast, it becomes dangerous. In the darkness the rejected psychic energy festers, and it also attracts to itself other energies from other parts of the unconscious. Then a personal anger can become fueled from a deeper source. In the undifferentiated world of the psyche the personal shadow merges with darker archetypal energies.

To venture behind the locked door in any basement is no easy task, nor should it be lightly undertaken. There are good reasons for keeping this door locked. Many monsters can be found lurking in the shadows behind it. Yet however much our dreamer delays, she knows that this is her destiny; she knows that someday she will have "to go in." Rarely do we voluntarily cross into the darkness of the unconscious. We are drawn, or pushed, by a force more potent than our own ego. We may try to avoid or run away from this deeper destiny, but we know its significance and how our life needs us to live it.

Understandably our dreamer is reluctant to unlock the door into the basement, but as she is leaving, "this huge ferocious beast with great teeth came after me." Possibly, if she had opened the door and looked the danger in the face, it would not have been so ferocious, for the power of the shadow is that it comes from behind and attacks us through our fear of the unknown. Just as children are afraid of the dark, we are afraid of our inner darkness. Consciousness lights up this darkness and so lessens its power. But in the great teeth of the dreamer's inner monster is more aggression than she can face, and so it comes charging after her as she runs away.

Then her monster changes form, for the unconscious is the master of metamorphosis. In the unconscious, images shift and change, appear and reappear in different guises. The monster's teeth become the grates on the front of the Volvo, and then the driver gets out. Emanating cruelty, she personifies an aspect of the shadow, and although "very dangerous," "she was in a form that was safe." In this way the unconscious presents the dreamer with her shadow in a form which she can relate to: first there is the nameless danger behind the locked door; then the ferocious beast; finally a cruel woman. As the energies of the unconscious come closer to consciousness, they take on a more human guise. Another friend's dream began with two children poking their fingers at a crocodile and then changed to the children dancing with a gorilla which had a human face. Eventually our dreamer will have to face the darkest monster within her, but her journey to this "heart of darkness" begins with her confronting her own personal cruelty, which the dream suggests she is now able to relate to and accept.

The final scene of this dream is very different, however, and points beyond the shadow into the realm of the Self. The dreamer is watching a parade in which "there is a beautiful green star with golden letters which spell 'ALCHEMY.'" In the heart the spark of the Self burns like a star, and this spark is the guide which we follow along the pathway that leads us Home. The more we aspire, the brighter this star glows and the more clearly it guides us. It shines through the clouds of our confusion and takes us to the birthplace of our own Self. That the color of the star is green is highly auspicious, for green is the color of growth and becoming, and for the Sufi it is the color of the realization of God.[8] The journey home is a natural unfolding. This was understood by the alchemists who called the inner light the *lumen natura* which "enlightens man as to the workings of nature and gives him an understanding of natural things."[9] We can only become what we are in the most natural core of our being, and just as a flower opens its petals towards the sun, so does the seeker open her heart to the Beloved.

The green star with golden letters spelling "ALCHEMY" images the natural alchemical process that will purify and transform the dreamer. This is the inner work of a lifetime and a journey of no end. But for our dreamer the doorway to the limitless world of the Self is the recognition of her own cruelty. It may appear paradoxical that our own darkness is the beginning of spiritual life, but this is what is meant in the Psalms by "The stone which the builders refused is become the head stone of the corner."[10] Our own shadow has immense transformative potential but is overlooked and disregarded by those who cannot humbly and sincerely accept their own nature. Spiritual and psychological work means taking a light into the darkness of oneself and loving and accepting what is found there. Most simple and yet most difficult, work upon the shadow lays the foundation for all further processes of inner transformation.

Alchemy and Psychology

Alchemy is the Western science of inner transformation. Carl Jung's first response to an alchemical text was "Good Lord, what nonsense." But later he realized the psychological importance of alchemy, for he discovered that what the alchemists were working with in their retorts and crucibles were not just chemical substances, but the projected contents of their own unconscious. The alchemical goal of turning lead into gold is fundamentally symbolic, and refers to the process of psychological transformation. The alchemical *opus* is what we would describe as "inner work," or working upon oneself, which aims to purify and transform the basic contents of the unconscious. The alchemical "gold" symbolizes a state of inner transformation which relates to an awareness of one's divine nature, what the alchemists called, among other names, the *lapis*, or philosopher's stone, and Jung termed the Self.

One of the important aspects of Jung's discovery was that in alchemical symbolism there exists a language that describes the processes of inner transformation. This transformation happens in the world of the psyche, which is a world of images; thus, the language of alchemy is a language of images, a language of symbols. Alchemical symbolism also appears in the dreams of individuals who are engaged in their own inner work, allowing the unconscious to communicate to the conscious mind and inform it of changes taking place in the depths. Through the work of Jung we are able to revalue this almost forgotten, symbolic language, and thus listen to and understand the voice of the psyche.

However, although Jung may have rediscovered this symbolic language for modern psychology, Sufis have always known about the inner processes of alchemy. A great twelfth-century Sufi, al-Ghazzâlî, titled one of his most important books *The Alchemy of Happiness*. Moreover, the Arabic word for 'stone' is associated with the word for 'hidden, forbidden', and, according to the Sufis, the stone is the essence which is so powerful that it can transform whatever comes into contact with it. This relates to Jung's concept of the Self, and the idea that it is the philosopher's stone, the Self, that effects the whole process of alchemical/psychological transformation.

For the wayfarer on the path the process of alchemical transformation takes place fueled by aspiration and meditation. And although one's spiritual journey is always a solitary path—it is the journey "of the alone to the Alone"—the Sufi is in the hands of the teacher and in the company of other wayfarers, as is imaged in the following dream:

> The group is at a school for turning base metal into silver. The basic material is black earth which is swept up and sifted and finally a silver metal dust appears. We are all trying to

> make silver bowls from this stuff in our own way. Then I am taken aside and shown the secret way of doing this. You take a blank white sheet and spread the metal dust over the sheet five times. Then you clamp the sheet between two bowl molds and squeeze. Then you take the rough bowl and polish and polish till it shines.

The alchemical process normally turns base matter, lead, into gold. But in this dream the "base metal" is being turned into silver, which is significant in that silver is symbolically feminine; for it is the longing, the feminine side of love, the cup waiting to be filled, that takes the Sufi to God. This cup is the "silver bowl" of the dream, which must be made in the workshop of the heart.

The dream's image of "black earth" as the "basic material" evokes the alchemical notion of the *prima materia,* which must be found before the inner process can commence. The *prima materia* is that which is rejected and considered waste:

> This Matter lies before the eyes of all; everybody sees it, touches it, loves it, knows it not. It is glorious and vile, precious and of small account, and is found everywhere.[11]

Psychologically, the *prima materia* is the shadow, the undifferentiated contents of the unconscious that form the basis of the *opus* and is most often experienced in the form of projections, or unexpected moods or reactions. For in such forms unconscious feelings express themselves; the unconscious 'spills over' into our conscious life. The alchemical process is concerned with the differentiation and integration of the unconscious, and therefore this process cannot begin without the individual's "getting hold of" the mercurial contents of his psyche.

Whenever one finds oneself reacting with more feeling or emotion than is justified by the objective situation, then something has "come up" from the unconscious, and there is an opportunity to "get hold" of the *prima materia.* It is, therefore, important to try to differentiate between what belongs to the external situation and is an appropriate *response,* and what is primarily a *reaction,* something belonging to one's own unconscious patterns and projections which have been 'triggered' by the external situation. And because such unconscious material is not valued by the conscious mind, and is often considered humiliating, it is left lying around in the dusty corners of our lives, in unpleasant or humiliating incidents, where it can be found by the simple act of "sweeping." The *opus* commences with our looking into those dusty corners and valuing what is found there, however disagreeable it may appear. The very act of taking notice of one's moods or reactions, and trying to understand their source, allows consciousness to begin to grasp and thus "work" with the unconscious.

For most people today, the alchemical workshop is in the field of personal relationships. While the alchemists projected their unconscious into the mysterious processes of chemistry, we project our psychic contents most easily onto our relationships. Personal relationships form the groundwork for most psychological inner work, for it is here that we appear to have least conscious control of ourselves, and where the unconscious finds greatest room for expression. In fact, many personal relationships are wrecked by the explosions of the unconscious. Within our society, the nuclear family and the importance attached to romantic love have placed immense pressure on personal relationships, with the result that they are often the battleground of the unconscious. Yet this battleground can become a workshop for the transmutation of the human being, for it is in the feelings we project on to our relationships that we have the most direct access to the unconscious. Here lies the *prima materia* for the *opus* which can be a human being's most important work. Here is the "black earth" of this alchemical dream which, when swept up and sifted, becomes silver.

"Black earth" relates specifically to the first phase of the alchemical process, the *nigredo* (*terra nigra*), which "has its parallels in the individuation process, in the confrontation with the shadow."[12] From a psychological perspective, the work of transformation begins with the shadow, which in alchemy is "the black earth in which the gold or *lapis* is sown like the grain of wheat."[13] Therefore, just as for a previous dreamer the path began with the recognition of her own cruelty, so in this dream the *opus* begins with sweeping up the "black earth."

However, "sweeping" also has a specific Sufi association, for Sufis are known as "sweepers" or the "dustbins of humanity." In one dream, Irina Tweedie met a great Sufi with his followers, and when she asked a disciple if he was a Bishop she was told:

> "No, no ... he is on the same Line as Bhai Sahib [Irina Tweedie's teacher], and he is very fond of joking; speaking of himself and those like him

> he will say: 'Nous autres balayeurs'" (which means in French: "we sweepers").
>
> "Oh, I see!" I exclaimed, "it is because they clean the hearts of the people!"
>
> "Precisely!" the disciple said.[14]

And the idea of the Sufi as a "dustbin" is reflected in another dream told in our Sufi group:

> I had two dustbins full of rubbish. The teacher came along and emptied my two dustbins into his one dustbin, and walked off.

On the Sufi path the process of inner purification happens through the work of the wayfarer and the grace of the teacher.

After the black earth is swept up, silver dust appears. Then comes the stage of making silver bowls and the dreamer is "taken aside and shown the secret way of doing this": "You take a blank white sheet and spread the metal dust over the sheet five times." The "blank white sheet" suggests the state of inner purification that comes from working on the shadow, and corresponds in the alchemical process to the *albedo*, the "whitening." The "whitening" is also the light, the illumination that follows the darkness of the *nigredo*, for out of the confrontation and acceptance of the shadow is born a purified state of consciousness.

That the metal dust is spread over the sheet five times is very significant, for five is the number of mankind or humanity—we have five senses—and in order for an inner transformation to be fully realized, it must be lived. An inner realization that remains just an idea is never fully integrated; it has to become part and parcel of our daily life. This is reflected in the fact that, according to Jung, the final stage in the alchemical process, after the "whitening," is the "reddening":

> In order to come alive it must have "blood," it must have what the alchemists call the *rubedo*, the "redness" of life.[15]

On the Sufi path this "reddening" is effected through being "in the world but not of the world," a practice in which the wayfarer lives an ordinary everyday life, bringing up a family, working, and yet at the same time keeps the inner attention focused inwardly on the heart and the remembrance of the Beloved. In this way the silver is spread five times, and then molded by the grace of God from above, and by the experience of the world from below. The coming together of the two worlds is a central aspect of the Sufi way.

In the dream the making of the bowl follows the three major stages of the alchemical *opus*, the *nigredo*, the *albedo*, and the *rubedo*. But the "rough bowl" made by this process should then be polished and polished "till it shines." This image of "polishing" refers to the Sufi notion that the heart is a mirror which the lover polishes and polishes with his aspiration and longing, until the mirror of the heart can reflect the true light of the Beloved:

> Whether your lot be glory or disgrace, be pure of both hatred and love of self. Polish your mirror, and perhaps that sublime beauty from the regions of mystery will shine in your breast—just as it did for the prophets. And then, with your heart illuminated by that splendor, the

> secret of the beloved will no longer be concealed from you.[16]

Finding the Prima Materia

Finding the *prima materia* is the essential first step in the *opus*, and yet the alchemists describe it as notoriously difficult to get hold of. The difficulty of finding one's shadow is that the shadow is what is rejected, dismissed, and left in the darkness. But one of the effects of spiritual practices is to energize the contents of the unconscious, so that what had been repressed begins to come to the surface of consciousness. Once we are sincere and prepared to cross over into the shadowlands of the underworld, then an opportunity will present itself for this inner work to commence. The following psychological situation and dream offer an example of "getting hold" of the *prima materia* and the transformative potential this offers:

> First I was aware of resentment towards my parents, and instead of just repressing it I decided to become more aware of it. This released a lot of energy and a dream followed:
>
> I am up a tower that is beginning to crumble, but I see a vast, beautiful landscape. Then I go down the tower and am shown a large, gold eagle.

For a long time this man had felt his resentment towards his parents, but had repressed these feelings whenever they began to surface. He had regarded these feelings as useless. We have all experienced the violence and destruction when uncontained feelings explode in anger, or surface in poisonous remarks. If these dark feelings have no place in our outer life, and cannot be expressed creatively, what are we to do? The dreamer could have expressed his resentment, become angry with his parents, which might have created a temporary release. But he knew that his parents would not have understood, or even been capable of understanding his resentment. Accepting or understanding his feelings would have forced them to confront and begin to work on their own shadow, and this work is not for everyone. Jung commented that it can be totally inappropriate, even dangerous, to confront somebody with a psychological truth which he does not wish to or indeed cannot accept and integrate. Truth can be not only useless but cruel; and "when there is complete unconsciousness, don't say anything. The shock would be too great."[17]

The alchemists stressed that their *opus* requires a container, the alchemical vessel. Psychologically this vessel is an inner attitude of commitment to confront and accept whatever is found within oneself; it must be a vessel strong enough to contain the conflict when the shadow comes into the light and "one becomes two." The pressing need to know oneself and find the light hidden in darkness provides this container, but without it one's demons are best left undisturbed. I was once asked by a woman at a workshop why she didn't dream. I replied that possibly she was so integrated and led such a balanced life that there was no need for her to dream. She knew that this was not the case. Then I suggested that maybe she didn't want to deal with what her dreams would tell her. She said, "Of course I want to know what my dreams tell me." "Are you really prepared to spend the next five or more years discovering and accepting all your negative qualities, your failings and unpleasant feelings?" "Oh no!" she responded. I admired her honesty. Without the right attitude it is best to leave the door to the underworld closed. One should never open this door just for the sake of curiosity, or without the commitment to work with what one finds within oneself. There are good reasons why our shadow was born, and why for many people the underworld belongs only to myths and fairy tales.

But the dreamer felt the need, the prompting, to allow his feelings to surface. Instinctively he knew they were the lead that could be turned into gold. Although it was inappropriate to tell his parents how he truly felt, he was no longer going to repress his resentment. Then, one day as he was cycling to work, once again the feelings of resentment surfaced. Rather than repressing it, he decided to look at it, to become conscious of it. Suddenly the whole energy flow in his body changed, and an enormous psychological shift took place. He had made the decision to work with the contents of his unconscious; in other words, the alchemical *opus* had begun. This actual decision in itself may have been the trigger that "released a lot of energy," as psychic energy held repressed in the unconscious began to flow into consciousness.

"Awareness" is the most fundamental quality of consciousness, and in being aware of his resentment he formed a connection between consciousness and the unconscious through which the energy in the unconscious could begin to be integrated into consciousness. One of Jung's major discoveries was that the very process of being *aware* of the contents of the unconscious has a magical effect, vastly speeding up the transformative processes of the psyche. Jung believed that individuation actually happens to everyone,[18] but for most people it takes place only in the unconscious and is very, very slow. They hardly even realize that gradual changes are happening within them, changes that take them through the various stages of life and eventually prepare them for death. But the moment the individual takes the step of becoming aware of what is taking place in the unconscious, a spark of consciousness crosses over into the darkness. It is as if this spark then ignites an immeasurably faster process of individuation, and it is this "speeded-up" process which we tend to refer to by the psychological term "individuation." The participation of consciousness with the unconsciousness is like a chemical catalyst. This is when the *opus* really commences, and the dream that the man was given after he began to look at his feelings of resentment offers a clear indication of the psychological process he initiated.

The dreamer's tower can be read as a symbol of isolated consciousness, a consciousness separated from the reality of his own feelings and their connection to life. There is a tarot card, "The Tower of Destruction,"[19] in which the tower images isolation and a state of psychological imbalance, being cut off from other human beings and also from the earth. A masculine symbol, it represents a mental attitude that can serve as a protection against chaos, particularly the chaos of the unconscious. Yet all too often does this self-protection end as a prison for the inhabitant, who becomes isolated, cut off from his own feelings and the flow of life. But once the individual begins to acknowledge what had been repressed and denied, the tower crumbles. Reality with all its richness and confusion takes over from the ivory tower of our imagined self.

Moreover, this dreamer is shown two very auspicious symbols, "a vast, beautiful landscape" and "a large, gold eagle." The vast, beautiful landscape suggests new psychological horizons, no longer limited by the restriction of repression. Dreams often show these new landscapes, sometimes seen through a doorway, archway, or window. For as we accept and integrate the contents of the unconscious there is an expansion of consciousness; as we work upon our conditioning, complexes, and shadow dynamics, so they release the psychic energy which had been stored within them. Aspects of our own self which had been locked behind the doors of the unconscious become part of our conscious life. Thus in dreams people find new rooms in their house, or even find a doorway to a whole new floor, possibly an attic which they did not know existed. And because the shadow contains not only the dark side of the ego, but also unlived potential, so that too becomes integrated, with the result that daily life becomes richer and more creative.

Psychological work is *real* and really changes a human being. We have become conditioned to believe that life can only improve externally, usually in quantitative, material terms: more is better. But real meaning and fulfillment come from the inner and not the outer world; and deep psychological work results in lasting change that is not subject to the whims of fortune. As the inner darkness is transmuted, so more light comes into the psyche, and then the *quality* of life changes. External situations may change, as the individual discovers new potential that requires expression. But one's physical situation may also remain unchanged, and yet be perceived differently, just as we all know that the same street can be beautiful or nondescript depending on our mood. The Zen saying,

"Before enlightenment, chop wood and carry water. After enlightenment, chop wood and carry water," expresses this truth about inner change. From the outside life may appear to be the same, but the experience is very different.

The dream of the crumbling tower has another symbol of transformation, "a large, gold eagle." The eagle, thought to be able to look unblinking into the full light of the sun, is a solar symbol, and in alchemy it signifies the philosophical gold. The dreamer's image of the "large, gold eagle" symbolizes the transformation of the instinctual energy of the unconscious that results from working with the *prima materia*. This gold eagle is the same as the *lapis* which is both the beginning and the end of the *opus*. It is the spiritual principle within the dreamer that initiates the process, forcing him out of the tower and into contact with the unconscious. And this eagle is also the goal, his own divine Self which he will meet at the end of the path.

From something so simple and easily overlooked as his resentment towards his parents, the work of a lifetime commences, the ancient alchemical *opus* of turning lead into gold. The gold eagle, the higher energy of the Self, is present at the very beginning, pushing the dreamer to change his attitude and allow the fluid, amorphous energy of the unconscious into consciousness, opening the doorway into the underworld of his own initiation and transformation. Each seeker will find the *prima materia* where it is least expected, but even in this initial stage we are guided by the light of the Self and the deep need within us to realize what is infinitely precious, our divine nature.

THE PAIN OF THE COLLECTIVE SHADOW

All is sweet that comes from the Beloved's side—
It is never bitter if you taste it with care.

Abdul Latif[1]

THE SHADOW OF DISBELIEF

The spiritual path takes the seeker into the very depths of the psyche, where the wayfarer must confront not only the personal but also the collective shadow. Our patriarchal culture has resulted in the wounding of Mother Earth, and also in the wounding of the feminine principle itself. A woman howling with anguish and despair, her face hidden by her tears, haunts the pathways of the unconscious. This archetypal figure is not as visible as the ecological disaster that threatens our planet. She belongs to the intangible inner world, a reality we have almost totally rejected as valueless. But anyone entering this inner reality will soon encounter this figure and feel her pain.

The tragic plight of our own feminine nature was powerfully imaged for me in a dream I had soon after I began my study of Jungian psychology:

> I was walking down a street and on the right-hand side there was a magnificent new hospital, gleaming white, with doctors walking in. But on the left-hand side of the street was a totally different picture. There were cattle trucks, full of men and women, reminiscent of those that took

> the Jews to concentration camps. The people there were unwashed, undernourished, and standing in their own feces. For a long time nobody had cleaned out these trucks, but most tragic of all was the fact that the men and women there had got so used to this situation that they no longer cared or expected anything else.

The right-hand side in a dream symbolizes consciousness. We are surrounded by the wonders of our masculine consciousness. Each time I fly in an airplane I marvel at the technology that can lift so much machinery and so many people above the clouds and fly them around the world. Such wonders are not to be despised, but they have been bought at a price. In our fascination with the world of science and its tangible results, we have starved and neglected the inner feminine world. Feces symbolize creativity, for they are produced from within. But what do we do with our inner creativity? Unused, it pollutes us. And most tragic, we have even got used to this situation. The figures in the cattle trucks no longer expect anything else. We are starving and our hunger is all the more desperate because we do not even recognize it.

Why have drugs taken such a hold on the affluent West? Because our materialistic culture has created an inner vacuum. The hunger of the neglected feminine, the inner world of the soul, has become vicious and turned itself into a monstrous beast, a vampire-like shadow which sucks the blood of its people. The attraction of drugs, which destroy individuals and families and appeal to any psychological weakness, will never be stopped by force. Only when our culture has accepted the need for inner experience will drugs lose their fatal attraction. The inner world is no mere fantasy land, but a real and vital part of our human nature. In past ages dishonoring the gods brought down their wrath. We have not merely dishonored them; we have denied their existence.

For those who sincerely wish to work upon themselves, the most dominant collective shadow is this disbelief in the inner world itself. Because our culture views the external, physical world as the only reality, we have collectively negated the inner world. Furthermore, the imagination is our primary mode of access into the symbolic world; yet, over the centuries, it has been denigrated by being regarded as mere fantasy. Rather than being held holy, the symbolic world has become imaginary, the stuff of children's tales. We don't believe in dragons anymore and have even lost the ability to walk in a symbolic world. Over the past centuries this darkness of disbelief has grown in the unconscious. It can appear in the mockery of friends who do not honor your paying serious attention to the substance of dreams. In the collective unconscious it takes the form of a collective resistance to anyone who tries to work with the fabric of his dreams, learn the symbolic language of the psyche, and appreciate the real potential of the imagination.

Here lies the value of dreamwork within a group. As dreams are shared and valued, their substance becomes more real, the inner world more tangible. Some dreams must always remain private, for at times they speak secrets of the soul that are not for the ears of others. But most often the sharing of a dream with sympathetic friends helps to counteract this collective disbelief and reinforces a connection to the inner world.

In a dream the inner world talks to the world of consciousness. Speaking in the ancient language of images and symbols, the unconscious tells its stories. Sometimes these stories describe conflicts, joys, or difficulties that are purely personal. They tell of childhood patterns, complexes, or unresolved anger that have meaning only to the dreamer. But there are other dreams that express the collective song of the soul. They tell of archetypal, mythic happenings which are both personal and universal. When these dreams are told within a group a deep sharing takes place. For then the spoken images resonate not just within the conscious ear of the listener, but also within the sacred spaces of the soul. Psyche speaks to psyche; heart listens to heart. A door is opened into the symbolic interior, into the world of the gods, and through this doorway a music is heard that echoes and re-echoes. It awakens distant memories of when we walked as children upon the shore of the great ocean of life. Just as a child hears the roar of the sea within a sea shell, so we hear in such dreams the song of our own deepest nature.

HEALING A WOUNDED UNICORN

Heard with an open heart, a dream can touch the innermost places of the soul, can speak to the soul in its own language. When the following dream was told, a magic entered the room that made real the symbols whose song is normally drowned by the noise of our world.

> I enter a great cathedral-like building. Overhead is a high arched roof and around the building are sarcophagi with the stone figures of men and women. I come to one tomb on which lies the stone figure of a woman my age but with long, golden hair.
>
> I merge with this figure and at the same time am separate, looking on. At this moment a unicorn flies through the window. It is very bedraggled and forlorn-looking. Its mane is tangled and its horn is hanging, almost broken off. It pleads with me to help it, but I don't know how. The unicorn describes the herbs which it needs but I don't know how to get them. We look into each other's eyes for a long time. He is so sad. Then he flies off through the window and looking out I see that he has alighted in a field a little way down a hillside.

We all have within us such cathedrals and temples. Sometimes they have pillars of white marble, sometimes stained-glass windows through which the sun shines. In the unconscious we have these holy places, magnificent and sacred. We may live in small city rooms but in the inner world there are other dimensions which belong both to the present and to the long-distant past. These are the sacred memories we have carried from our real home. In the words of Tagore, "Thou hast made me endless, such is thy pleasure."[2] Entering such imaginal buildings, we feel awe at something within us far greater than the ego. We are touching the stones that are the foundations of our true being.

For our dreamer, her cathedral contains stone tombs. These are buried parts of herself. She does not live within her own sacred space, and so its inhabitants—the figures of wisdom, the priests and priestesses of her psyche—have turned to stone. The negative effect of the unconscious is to petrify, as in the myth of Medusa, whose snake-covered head turns everything that beholds it to stone. The White Witch in C.S. Lewis's *The Lion, The Witch and the Wardrobe* exhibits the same ice-cold power, filling her courtyard with the creatures of Narnia she has turned into stone. This is the archetypal dynamic of the devouring feminine, whether the *femme fatale* or the spider-mother who psychologically feeds on her children.

Stony-faced men and women who have lost contact with the warmth of their own feelings testify to the power of the witch. Personal feelings have been devoured by the cold abyss of the unconscious, which, having sucked their blood, has then left them empty and hard. But this process also happens in the depths of the psyche. When we stop relating to the ancient figures who inhabit this inner world, the warmth of feeling is withdrawn, and these figures too become cold and isolated. Warmth comes from consciousness (the theft of fire symbolizes the birth of consciousness). The further from consciousness we travel, the colder it becomes. The figures that we have left forgotten and abandoned in the temples of the imagination become stone sarcophagi, entombed in their own isolation.

Yet, as in the fairy tales, this magic can be reversed. The petrified figures can be freed from the spell that has held them. Just as the kiss awoke Sleeping Beauty, so love can always redeem and transform. If we love these inner figures, they will be healed and made whole. The inhabitants of the archetypal world need us; they need the light of consciousness and the warmth of love. If we speak to them with tenderness, their eyes will open and their deep wisdom will be at our service.

Our dreamer finds herself in front of one tomb with a figure much like herself, although the figure has long hair while her hair is short. She merges with this figure; she becomes one with this ancient part of herself. At that moment a unicorn comes flying in through the window, a unicorn that needs her help in order to be healed. The unicorn is a fabulous creature rich in symbolic meaning. It is a lunar animal, and yet its single horn has a masculine quality. Jung explored its symbolism in detail and found that it had no one symbolic meaning, but he associated it with the *spiritus mercurialis*, which is the very spirit of alchemical transformation.[3] According to legend the unicorn is tireless fleeing from pursuit, but will lay its head in the lap of a pure virgin. Thus it is the purity of the receptive feminine principle that is needed to integrate this powerful, transformative psychic energy. The energies of the unconscious can be wild and destructive, and woe be to him who tries to harness them for the power purposes of the ego, for personal gain or greed. But if the seeker has purity of heart and is receptive to the inner processes, this psychic energy can be creatively integrated. According to the alchemists, the unicorn was Christ. The energy of the Christ principle, or the Self (which is the prime force in the alchemical *opus*), will always be destructive to the desires of the ego and will foster the growth of the soul.[4]

Our dreamer's unicorn is also able to fly and thus has the qualities of Pegasus, the mythic flying horse. Pegasus was a winged horse which sprang from the blood of Medusa, when Perseus cut off her head. It thus symbolizes the transformation of the dark side of the feminine, of the petrifying forces of the Great Mother. Pegasus symbolizes the "innate capacity for spiritualization and for inverting evil into good."[5] Thus this unicorn has immense transformative potential. It is the spiritual force within the dreamer that, born out of the darkness, will carry her into the light.

But as the dreamer told her story, I felt such sadness at the forlorn plight of the unicorn. How had this magical beast become so neglected? This feeling was intensified a few minutes later when a six-year-old girl, who was also present at this meeting, described a vision she had had only a few nights previously. She had awakened to find at the end of her bed the most beautiful of unicorns, full of light and beauty. Her unicorn's horn was not broken, but shining and surrounded by a rainbow ring of light. And on the unicorn's back there rode a man of light. Such visions are a glimpse into the real inner world whose very substance is light, and in response to this vision, the teacher suggested that next time the young girl saw her unicorn she should talk to its rider, and so form a conscious connection with her own inner man of light.

That afternoon synchronicity presented us with these two unicorns, adding poignancy to the question of how the dreamer's unicorn had become so neglected. The six-year-old girl still lived in the magical world of her own inner nature. The archetypal world was for her, as for many children, a living reality. She had not yet been told that dragons don't exist nor had her own magical self "fade into the light of common day."[6] In "Ode: Intimations of Immortality" Wordsworth describes this sad transition:

There was a time when meadow, grove,
  and stream,
The earth, and every common sight,
    To me did seem
  Apparelled in celestial light,
The glory and the freshness of a dream.
It is not now as it hath been of yore;—
  Turn whereso'er I may,
    By night or day,
The things which I have seen I now can
  see no more.[7]

As the child goes to school and enters the world of competition and peer pressure, unicorns slowly become less real. "Dragons live forever but not so little boys," and no doubt it is necessary that the growing child step out of the ocean of the unconscious onto the dry land of consciousness. As the ego develops, the child ceases to be immersed in the archetypal world. Yet the danger is that the magical world is not just left to be returned to later in life, but is rejected and locked in the darkness of the shadow. And it is even more tragic when we have lost touch with the faculty of the imagination, which would enable us to open the locked door and enter into this world.

Our culture has so firmly rejected the inner world that as the child grows into adulthood, its own inner reality can easily become part of the collective shadow. It is then that the unicorn loses its light, and its horn hangs almost broken off. Our dreamer's unicorn had been infected by this collective shadow and had almost lost its transformative potential. It needed herbs to be healed.

But how does one heal a unicorn? The dreamer didn't know what to do. If we live in a world that doesn't believe in unicorns, is it likely that we would know how to heal them? And even when the unicorn told the dreamer exactly what herbs it needed, she didn't know where to find them.

But why did the unicorn come to her unless it knew she was able to help it? These archetypal figures have a deep wisdom and understanding. The unicorn knows more about the workings of the inner world than the conscious mind of the dreamer. It knows she can heal its wounded horn. She is the virgin in whose lap it can lay its weary head.

In the inner life of a woman the term "virgin" has a particular significance: a virgin is a woman who is true to her own inner feminine nature, the Goddess within ("A girl belongs to herself while she is a virgin.... She is 'One in herself'"[8]). Our dreamer's healing powers are within her deeper feminine self which until now has been buried and petrified. This is the golden-haired woman on the sarcophagus she merges with and yet is also separate from. It is after this merging that the unicorn flies down to her, knowing that if she can reawaken the golden-haired figure the unicorn will be healed. It is this figure who understands the healing powers of herbs, which form part of the ancient mystery of the feminine. Herbs belong to nature, to Mother Earth herself, and their use belongs to the primordial knowledge of woman. Similarly, poison, which is the dark use of such knowledge, belongs to the "natural magic" of Hecate, the goddess of the underworld.

Thus the dream suggests that if the dreamer can enter her own sacred inner space and reconnect with the feminine power within, she will be able to heal the very principle of spiritual transformation which has been wounded. But the dream also makes the important statement that this inner descent, the merging within, must be balanced by the presence of an observing consciousness. When she merges with the stone figure she also remains separate, observing. In the myth of Perseus, the hero can only look at the face of Medusa in the reflection of his shield. Reflection symbolizes consciousness:

> "Reflection" should be understood not simply as an act of thought, but rather as an attitude. It is a privilege born of human freedom in contradistinction to the compulsion of natural law. As the word itself testifies ("reflection means literally 'bending back'"), reflection is a spiritual act that runs counter to the natural process; as an act whereby we stop, call something to mind, form a picture, and take up a relation to and come to terms with what we have seen. It should therefore be understood as an act of *becoming conscious.*[9]

Our reflective powers not only separate us from the animal world, they also allow us to look into the depths of the unconscious without being assimilated back into that primal world. It is the attitude of reflection, of being a witness or inner observer, that counterbalances the devouring powers of the unconscious. It stops one from being turned into stone.

At the end of the dream the unicorn can be seen standing in a field. It is to be hoped that its sad plight will impress upon the dreamer the importance of the task before her. This is what Jung termed "a big dream," a milestone in the life of the dreamer. The dream is a cry from the depths, and if the dreamer heeds this cry and finds within herself the feminine wisdom that will heal the unicorn, then the powerful energies of spiritual transformation will begin to change the very structure of her being. The unicorn carries the secrets of this transformation, and for the dreamer it will be the most wondrous of journeys, one that will take her far beyond the boundaries of her own consciousness: "We know how it begins, but we never know how it will end. It is the way leading into the infinite."[10]

God Enters Through a Wound

The dream of the wounded unicorn touches upon the primal mystery that it is our wounds that take us home. It is because of our wounds, our pain and our sadness, that we turn away from the outer world and trace the thread of our own darkness back to its source. This thread leads us through the barriers of pain to the place of our own healing; in the very process of making this journey, the light of consciousness which we carry with us transforms our darkness. The individual who arrives at the source is very different from the person who set out upon the quest. During the course of this journey we have to accept and integrate what we find within us—our pain and our anger and all the many forms which our darkness has taken. We will find the thief, the murderer, and the prostitute. We will see both the hurt we have caused others and the hurt we have caused ourselves. We will have to accept ourselves as we really are, as our own naked self. Then this naked self will be the chalice into which His wine can be poured.

One of the foundations of the Sufi path is the understanding that this whole process of transformation takes place in the heart, fueled by love. The heart is the alchemical vessel, in which we place the substance of the shadow, which is then transformed through the fire of love. It is for this reason that Simone Weil wrote: "We must not wish for the disappearance of our troubles, but the grace to transform them." In the following dream the dreamer's feminine self is deeply wounded, but it is this wound that leads to the opening of her heart.

> I am with another woman. A man comes and fires a gun into my heart. I am taken to a stone and lie there while women mourn about me. Then I see that the skin about my left breast hangs down, like a flap, and underneath are the petals of a flower.

The dreamer had been very hurt by her father as a child and thus this dream carries powerful personal associations. The father carries the first image of the masculine within the psyche of the child, and our dreamer's primary masculine imprint had been a wounding of the heart. Yet this dream not only embraces the personal, but points beyond the personal into the archetypal. Her wound results in her being carried to a stone, the most ancient of altars and a symbol of the Self. There, in the depths of her own primal Self, she is mourned by women. Thus the feminine mourns the wounding it has suffered at the hands of the masculine.

In the depths of the psyche of both men and women the feminine feels betrayed, ravaged, and misunderstood. This archetypal wounding will manifest for each of us in its own individual way. It can be a wounded feeling, an inner anger, or painful vulnerability. It can manifest as an inability to relate, an undervaluing of one's creativity, or a woman's disbelief in her own feminine wisdom. The collective manifests in the personal, and we can often trace a personal conflict back to an archetypal source. In this dream a personal and an archetypal pain are clearly related, but the dream points beyond the pain to its deeper significance. To quote the English visionary artist, Cecil Collins, "God enters through a wound"; underneath the skin that covers her heart the dreamer finds the petals of a flower.

There is a flowering that can only occur through pain. This is the flowering of the heart. Pain takes us beyond the surface world of the ego into the realm of the soul. Keats describes this world as a vale of tears which is also a vale of soulmaking. There is a suffering that purifies and transforms, destroying the structures of the ego so that the vaster world of the Self can be made visible:

> There was an artist once, and he painted a picture. Other artists had colours richer and rarer, and painted more notable pictures. He painted his with one colour. There was a wonderful red glow on it; and people went up and down saying, "We like the picture, we like the glow."
>
> The other artists came and said, "Where does he get his colour from?" They asked him; and he smiled and said, "I cannot tell you"; and worked on with his head bent low.
>
> And one went to the Far East and bought costly pigments, and made a rare colour and

> painted, but after a time the colour faded. Another read in the old books, and made a colour rich and rare, but when he had put it on the picture it was dead.
>
> But the artist painted on. Always the work got redder and redder, and the artist grew whiter and whiter. At last one day they found him dead before his picture, and they took him up to bury him. The other men looked about in all the pots and crucibles, but they found nothing they had not.
>
> And when they undressed him and put his grave-clothes on him, they found above his left breast the mark of a wound—it must have been there all his life, for the edges were old and hardened; but Death, who seals up all things, had drawn the edges together, and closed it up.
>
> And they buried him. And still the people went about saying, "Where did he find his colour from?"
>
> And it came to pass that after a while the artist was forgotten—but the work lived.[11]

In offering oneself as a sacrifice on the altar of the heart, one does not seek suffering, but chooses not to avoid it. One allows the powerful energies of the Self to burn away the impurities within the psyche. For every new birth there must be a breaking down of the old, and old patterns are best washed away with tears. Yet finally, the opening of the heart is always an act of grace. It is given. Suffering unlocks the door which is then opened by the hand of God. Abû Sa'îd al-Kharrâz describes this paradox of the effortless path:

> By suffering, none attained
> the treasure of mystic union;
> and, strange to say, without suffering,
> none beheld that treasure.[12]

Spiritual life is free; like the sun it shines on all alike. Yet, at the same time, whatever you want you must pay for. If you want the truth you must pay, not with money, but with the blood of your heart. As a friend was told when he first came to our group, "Here no money is charged; instead you will pay with yourself." Mirabai describes this same bargain:

> I have bought God, I have bought God.
> The bargain was easy.
> I gave myself completely
> And got him completely in return.[13]

The Power of the Goddess

The pain of the wounded woman dominates our collective shadow. Our patriarchal culture has raped and pillaged, leaving inner and outer desolation. Man's fear of the feminine has resulted in her instinctual wisdom being burnt at the stake and lost, buried deep in the unconscious. So powerful has been this collective repression that today not only men but also women are frightened of their own instinctual power. In the following dream the dreamer, a woman, encounters the Great Goddess Maria, and yet is apprehensive of her power:

> I am in a circus, in the arena. There is a central post which holds up the tent. Many

> people are moving around the post, like in a merry-go-round. Then I see a woman who is very, very beautiful, the most beautiful woman I have ever seen. She has stars on her ears and fingers. She is called Maria. Then in the middle of the arena there are some tigers. Maria and a male member of our Sufi group are quite happy playing with the tigers. Then the tigers go outside; but after a while they come back and I have to let them in. I see them first through a glass wall and am a bit apprehensive.

The dreamer meets the Goddess Maria in the circus arena, under the tent. The tent and its central post are ancient Sufi symbols, for the Sufi teacher, the sheikh, is the post, the link between heaven and earth which provides a protected space for the disciple to come closer to God. And in this dream the "members of the group" are "moving around the post, like in a merry-go-round," suggesting the circular path towards wholeness. The spiritual path is not a linear progression; the Truth is not separate from the seeker. Rather the path is a spiral journey of uncovering what is hidden within us. I once had a dream in which, together with other members of the group, I was being led round and round in circles by the teacher. In the dream there was a frustration about not going anywhere, but when I awoke I laughed at myself because I remembered that there is nowhere to go:

> We shall not cease from exploration
> And the end of all our exploring
> Will be to arrive where we started
> And know the place for the first time.[14]

In this dream of meeting the Goddess Maria, the arena is a powerful symbol, for the Sufi, once committed to the path, is taken into love's arena to do battle with the ego, the *nafs*. And the words of the Roman gladiators, *"Ave. Operator, morituri te salutant"* ("Hail, Emperor, those about to die salute you"), are appropriate to the Sufi, for in that arena the ego is to die, reflecting a saying ascribed to the Prophet, that one has to die before one dies.

To die before one dies is the death of the ego, the "I" that separates us from the experience of divine unity. But this "death" is not the obliteration of the ego, for one cannot live in this world without it. Here one needs to have an individual identity; otherwise conscious life would be impossible: you would not know that you were separate from anyone or anything else. You and your neighbor would be the same, you and a table would be identical! Only in the state of the *unio mystica* does the ego disappear completely. In this state of union with God there is no individual identity, but a state of total oneness, as the individual is absorbed into the whole. Coming out of this mystical state one returns to the ego with all of its painful limitations. In love's arena the ego is dissolved and transformed so that it remains surrendered to the Higher Self and to God. For the disciple this transformation is experienced as a death, a painful process of dying to this world and the ego's desires, in order that one may fully awaken to the presence of the Beloved.

There, in the arena, the dreamer meets the Great Goddess known in the West as Maria, or the Virgin Mary. "The most beautiful woman I have ever seen," she is adorned with stars, reflecting her archetypal nature, and she is playing with tigers. The tiger is a vehicle of the Goddess (the Goddess is frequently depicted as riding on the back of a tiger), and is often associated with her dark side, the terrible Goddess. The tiger symbolizes her power, her undifferentiated primordial energy, which is the aspect of the Goddess most repressed in our patriarchal culture. This quality of the Goddess is both beautiful and terrible, as is encapsulated in William Blake's poem, "The Tyger":

> Tyger! Tyger! burning bright
> In the forests of the night,
> What immortal hand or eye
> Dare frame thy fearful symmetry?

This is the primal power of the feminine of which men are most afraid. And in this dream this power is emphasized by there being more than one tiger. Moreover, it must be integrated by the dreamer: "I have to let them in." Understandably, she is "a bit apprehensive." Like many women, she is frightened of her own feminine power.

But her fear of her own instinctual power is not just a result of our patriarchal shadow. This archetypal energy belongs to the amoral depths of the unconscious. Just like tigers in the jungle, the archetypes are awesome but impersonal forces of nature, each following nature's amoral and impersonal laws. Integrating these energies places tremendous responsibility and an ethical obligation upon the individual. The consciousness of the individual needs to add the dimension of ethical, human values to these numinous powers. Then the energy of the unconscious may be integrated beneficially, rather than swamping or distorting consciousness with raw power. We have to take responsibility for our own power.

The ethical responsibility demanded by the images of the unconscious is reflected in a more personal dream which followed this archetypal dream. It illustrates the subtle relationship between the collective and the personal unconscious, showing how an experience of an archetype required the dreamer to look closely at an aspect of her shadow:

> There are two men, one of whom wants to use me as a prostitute. I don't really want to, but an unknown woman is there who says that it is O.K.; she often does it, she just thinks about something else.

Portrayed in sexual imagery, this dream describes a personal conflict within the dreamer, and one that is also a central part of our patriarchal culture: the woman allowing herself to be used by a man. In this dream there are two men and two women, suggesting the marriage quaternio, yet in this case the sexual union would not represent integration, as the woman is being "used." She is prostituting her own feminine self, her inner integrity, to the masculine. For just as a woman may outwardly allow herself to be used by a man, so does this drama happen inwardly, as the inner feminine sells herself to masculine values.

How many women have allowed masculine, goal-oriented values to dominate and guide them? How often do women prostitute their inner feminine integrity, their sense of relatedness and wholeness, to fit into a culture based upon ego-centered greed and rational principles, principles that are causing such ecological damage to our own Mother Earth? In joking seriousness a woman recently told me that in her experience of the American culture a woman is free to do anything she wants, as long as it is masculine.

In this dream, the image of prostitution suggests that the dreamer does not respect the Goddess within. Significantly, it is an "unknown woman," symbolizing a shadow figure, who "says it is O.K." and "often does it" without being fully aware of what she is doing—"she just thinks about something else." As ever, the shadow acts unconsciously, without taking full responsibility for its actions. Responsibility means consciousness, and the shadow often tries to limit our conscious awareness, pulling us into its murky world. Furthermore, because it is a part of us, it knows the easiest way to do this. Our shadow knows our weak spots, the arguments and suggestions that will most easily convince us.

When discussing this dream, the dreamer wanted to know what to do, which is again a masculine attitude towards resolving a problem. Instead, it was suggested that she just become aware of her relationship to the masculine, how she continually sacrificed part of herself. Her awareness of her inner dynamic would also mean taking responsibility for her own feminine self. A few days later she had a dream in which a tiger came and licked her face! After encountering the Goddess in the form of Maria, the dreamer needed to respect the Goddess within herself; she could no longer unconsciously prostitute herself. Then the energy of the Goddess was friendly towards her.

In order to live one's own primal power, one needs to become conscious of one's shadow, for the undifferentiated energy of the unconscious is only destructive when it manifests through the negative aspect of the psyche. Consciousness and responsibility protect us against the negative effect of life's primal energies. History gives too many examples of a collective energy causing destruction because individuals did not take personal responsibility, but "looked the other way," as when ordinary German citizens pretended to be unaware of the concentration camps and the Nazis' "final solution" for the Jews.

The spiritual path takes us deep into the unconscious where we will find both collective shadows and the awesome power of the archetypes. On this journey consciousness is our light and our protector; but as we go deeper within, so our ethical responsibility needs to increase. We cannot afford to allow our shadow to remain unnoticed, but need to be aware of our failings and limitations as well as the numinous wonder of our inner self.

THE DANCE OF THE WARRIOR

The pain of the wounded feminine dominates the world of the shadow. But for a man the confrontation with the instinctual world can connect him with another archetype that now carries the darkness of the shadow, that of the warrior. The following dream images a process of transformation that takes the dreamer into the primal world of the warrior and thus into contact with his essential nature:

> I am staring a black panther in the face. Then I find myself in Africa, holding a spear and dancing a tribal dance. Then I find myself in an

> American Indian dance. Then I am back in my mother's womb and am being born. Then I myself am giving birth.

This dream begins with a full confrontation with the dark instinctual forces imaged by a black panther. These forces of the unconscious do not belong to the civilized world; they follow the amoral laws of the jungle. To the world of consciousness this primal power can seem a threat, for like the panther it is not conditioned by the duality of good and bad. It follows its own natural laws, and *is itself.* As our society has become more and more civilized, we have failed to integrate this energy, and it has taken on the darkness of our own ignorance. In order to return to the roots of our own being we have to enter this darkness. Folklore says that if you stare a wild animal in the eyes it will not attack you, and this is the best way to encounter the wild animal within.[15] The full glare of consciousness disarms the shadow and allows its energy to be transformed.

American Indians learned to consciously identify with their "power animal," and were thus able to tune into this source of power within themselves. Illness could be caused by someone's losing contact with his power animal, and then the shaman would journey with him into the inner world to find this animal and thus reconnect him with his own source of instinctual power and inner healing. Our dreamer has found his own power animal, and it will lead him to his rebirth.

The dreamer was an American and Jung noted that for white Americans the shadow is frequently represented by a black person or an Indian.[16] These races carry the rejected, "primitive" side of the white people. Our dreamer goes to the African roots of the black man, to the root of his own shadow: "I find myself in Africa, holding a spear and dancing a tribal dance." Dance symbolizes integration and in this dance the dreamer becomes part of the dance of his own primitive masculine nature. He is honoring the warrior within.

The warrior archetype embraces the figure of the hero, the individual who succeeds in his quest. But these figures have been wounded by Western technology: no longer is there trial by sword or spear. Characters like Rambo exert a fascination but do they carry the honor and dignity of ancient warriors like Hector of Troy? Can Achilles be fully replaced by James Bond? The warriors of today may enact the myth of the individual fighting the collective powers of darkness, but where is the spiritual dimension of their quest? Rather than containing symbols of transformation, their stories are senseless tales of violence. The archetype of the warrior appears to have lost its spiritual dimension and has become just a gladiator battling animals in the arena of a decadent civilization.

Our cultural split between consciousness and the unconscious has compromised the warrior. Adolescent boys need the warrior's masculine energy to become men, as is witnessed in their instinctive attraction to knives and guns. But instead of true tests of strength, our culture provides them only with video games and the zapping of alien monsters.

The warrior archetype may have been repressed into the shadow, but its deeper purpose can be found in the unconscious. When myths describe physical battles, these are only images of an inner struggle. The greatest battle is to do battle with oneself. The greatest adventure and the most difficult task is to enter into the darkness of one's own being and to come to know oneself. The inner path will test one to the limits of one's endurance. The confrontation with the shadow itself requires true courage and determination, for then the seeker finds that his enemy is in his own heart. W.B. Yeats remarked: "Why should we honour those who die on the field of battle? A man may show as reckless a courage in entering into the abyss of himself."[17]

The sword of the warrior is needed for this inner battle; yet it should be a sword tempered with love. This blade is not cold and uncaring, not heedlessly destructive. It is like the sharp surgeon's blade that is at times needed to heal a diseased body. The warrior's sword must carry the wisdom of understanding and yet at the same time be able to be ruthless—to learn "to care and not to care."[18] The power of love has this dual dynamic. Like a powerful immune system it cares for the needs of the soul by destroying the crystalized patterns of the mind and the structures of the ego. It forces us to go beyond the limitations of our consciousness and embrace a greater wholeness. The processes of inner transformation take place only when one perseveres beyond the limits of one's seeming endurance. It is then that the enantidromia happens ("enantidromia" is a term Jung uses for "the emergence of the unconscious opposite in the course of time"[19]) and darkness turns into light. On the path one is tested until one thinks: "'What can happen—I cannot more than die—' and [if] one accepts it, then the test has been passed and one is ready for the high stage."[20]

Within the psyche of a woman the quality of ruthless perseverance belongs to the masculine part of herself, her inner warrior. It is he who gives the woman the strength of will that is necessary for one who wishes to travel on the loneliest of paths. In the myth of Eros and Psyche, a story of feminine individuation, Psyche must finally descend into the underworld. On this journey she is told that she will pass a drowning man who will implore her to save him. But she must not be moved even with pity for him. This necessary firmness and strength of will are echoed in many other fairy tales and myths, with the injunction not to turn around or answer. It is far easier for a man to focus on a distant goal and reject what is close at hand. For a woman this is the most difficult of tests, and she will need all her will power to pass it. But on the path one must always focus on the essentials, on the real purpose of the quest, for it will consume every ounce of energy we have. A woman needs this masculine one-pointedness and the resolution to continue to the very end. One friend had a dream in which she and the teacher were cowboys, riding off into the sunset, together but alone. The cowboy images the Western myth of the warrior, encapsulated in the saying "A man's got to do what a man's got to do." As an instinctual figure he embodies the dreamer's gut determination to pursue the quest for truth—the most exacting task but the only really worthwhile one.

In the dream of the black panther, the dreamer, dancing with a spear, integrates his own primal masculine energy, the energy necessary for the quest. First he is in an African dance, and then in an American Indian dance. As an American Indian he brings this energy into the landscape of his own life. Traditionally the American Indians lived instinctually and symbolically. Through mandala sand paintings, sweat lodges, and other rituals, they attuned themselves to the Great Spirit that flows through all of life. Rooted within themselves and the land, the Indians experienced both their inner and outer life as holy, governed by One Spiritual Power. Within this sacred wholeness they understood the deepest meaning of the warrior, as expressed in a Sioux prayer:

> I seek strength, not to be greater than my brother,
> But to fight my greatest enemy—myself.

The dreamer connects with this primal energy and is part of its dance.

The journey into the instinctual world is a journey back into the womb of the Great Mother. It is the hero's night-sea journey from which he will be reborn. This is the second birth, which is spiritual rather than physical:

> That which is born of the flesh is flesh; and that which is born of the Spirit is spirit.
>
> Marvel not that I said unto thee, Ye must be born again.
>
> The wind bloweth where it listeth, and thou hearest the sound thereof, but canst not tell whence it cometh, and whither it goeth: so is every one that is born of the Spirit.[21]

After the Indian dance our dreamer finds himself in his own mother's womb, and then he experiences being born. Our spiritual self is hidden in the darkness, in the rejected energy of the shadow. In order to become whole we must return "to the primitive roots of our being," for in our "civilized culture" our primitive nature is the place of our spiritual rebirth. In previous ages, when man was enslaved by his instincts, the spiritual quest may have required that the seeker turn away from the instinctual world and look upwards towards consciousness. Then the aspirant conquered his instinctual drives through will power; the ascetic fasted in the desert or sat naked in his mountain cave. But our Western drive towards the Promethean heights of consciousness has meant that our spiritual wholeness is to be found in our primitive self. Through the tribal dance of the warrior our dreamer is reborn as he really is, in his own essential wholeness.

The final image in this dream is the dreamer giving birth. This is the birth of the Self, the divine child which is none other than our own innermost being. Enlightenment is to give birth to something within oneself, something infinitely mysterious and yet infinitely simple. It is to know absolutely that you are a part of a greater whole and yet at the same time to know that you are the wholeness. The Self is this knowledge, a knowledge that does not belong to the mind but spreads from the heart until it forms part of every cell of the body, or "every part, every cell of the body becomes a heart."[22] At the beginning this knowledge comes just in glimpses, but it slowly infuses itself into the whole human being—nothing is excluded; every cell knows that it belongs. In the words of Ghalib, "Those who know are always drunk on the wine of the Self."[23]

From the darkness this child is born, and it is nourished on meditation and aspiration. Its cry is the sigh of the soul. When it opens its eyes it sees infinite horizons and directs our gaze thither. The birth of the Self is but the beginning of the real path, and as we walk this path, the Beloved merges into the lover until nothing is left. When the seeker has been found, He looks through the eyes of His child and sees the secrets of His Own heart.

THE ALCHEMICAL OPUS II: THE INNER PARTNER

The minute I heard my first love story
I started looking for you, not knowing
how blind that was.

Lovers don't finally meet somewhere.
They're in each other all along.

Rûmî[1]

Purification and the Inner Masculine

The alchemical *opus* begins with a process of inner purification, working upon the shadow. But behind the shadow stands the animus or anima, the contrasexual aspects of the psyche. For a woman, the animus is an unknown man who is her divine lover; for a man, his dark lady is a goddess. These mysterious figures are first known as the agents of love, and through their magic attraction we fall in love and are caught in the unconscious entanglements of romance. They bridge the personal and archetypal worlds, and in them we feel the fascinating power of the inner depths. Both the animus and the anima have negative qualities which belong to the shadow side of the personality; but they are important inner figures, for, like Dante's Beatrice, they can act as guides in the transpersonal realm. A good relationship with the animus or anima is of great value, for it can help the seeker on the spiritual path that leads beyond the ego to the Self.

However, Jung stresses that work on the shadow precedes any relationship with the animus or anima:

> The integration of the shadow, or the realization of the personal unconscious, marks the first stage in the analytic process, and without it a recognition of the anima and animus is impossible.[2]

In the following dream, this process is depicted. It images inner purification as an activity of cleaning, but what is born is a positive relationship to the dreamer's animus, her inner partner.

> I am cleaning a house with all the energy I have; I scrub, clean, and polish every room until it shines. None of the rooms have doors and I am aware that in the main room in the center of the house there is a man lying on a mattress on the floor and that he watches everything that I do. I am not disturbed by this but I just get on with my cleaning. My last task is to clean the toilet which is exactly opposite where the man lies. I put my heart and soul into this room in particular. The walls are tiled and I polish them so hard that I can't look at them; it is like trying to look straight into the sun. And then I notice with horror that the window above the toilet is slightly open and I think that some dust might fly in and that would disturb the man. Somehow I have to close the window, but it is extremely high up and there is no way I can reach it. I stand staring up at the window puzzling how I can close it when the man gets out of his bed and

> comes to me and puts his arms around me. I think how frail he is and yet what strength he has.
>
> He reminds me of Gandhi to look at, and he says to me, "From tomorrow I will share everything with you. If you have work I will share it. If the child cries in the night I will deal with it, and if you need love I will give you love."
>
> I feel as though a great burden has been lifted from my shoulders and I wake up thinking that this dream is about yesterday, today, and tomorrow.

The dream begins with intense cleaning activity imaging the work on the shadow. In the center of the house of the dreamer's psyche lies a man watching everything, yet not participating or helping the dreamer. She continues with her cleaning, finally putting her "heart and soul" into cleaning the toilet and the tiled walls of this room. In dreams the toilet has psychological significance as a space where one produces something out of oneself—a place of psychological creativity. Furthermore, the way the dreamer polishes the walls of the toilet adds a spiritual dimension to her cleaning, echoing the polishing of the mirror of the heart that reflects the divine light: "I polish them [the walls] so hard that I can't look at them; it is like trying to look straight into the sun."

However, a problem arises for the dreamer when she notices that "the window above the toilet is slightly open and I think that some dust might fly in and that would disturb the man," and this window is too high up for her to close. The need to close the window suggests the "well-sealed vessel" *(vas bene clausum)* that is necessary for the alchemical *opus*. For the process of inner transformation requires that the contents of the psyche be hermetically sealed in order "to protect what is within from the intrusion and admixture of what is without":

> Nothing enters into it [the stone] that did not come from it; since, if anything extraneous were to be added to it, it would at once be spoilt.[3]

Psychologically, this refers to the need to withdraw projections and to discriminate between what belongs to oneself and what belongs to another, for one can transform only the contents of one's own psyche, and the "intrusion and admixture" of external psychological material leads only to confusion. In fact, this need for a "well-sealed vessel" often results in a period of introversion as the individual withdraws from the outside world and "broods" on the contents of her own psyche.

But, alone, the dreamer is unable to close this window, for the power of discrimination within the woman's psyche belongs to the masculine, the animus. The animus provides the focus lacking in the "diffused awareness" of the feminine mode of consciousness. Irene de Castillejo describes the animus as a "torch-bearer," "holding aloft his torch to light my way":

> In a woman's world of shadows and cosmic truths he provides a pool of light as a focus for her eyes.[4]

The masculine consciousness of the animus is needed to create boundaries, which is different from the all-inclusive nature of the feminine. A positive relationship with the animus is necessary if a woman is to see the fine line that differentiates the contents of her own psyche from that which intrudes from outside.

Yet, as if in response to the dreamer's need for help to close the window, the male figure gets off his bed and "comes to me and puts his arms around me." Frail and yet full of strength, he reminds her of Gandhi, who, according to Marie-Louise von Franz, is a figure who often carries the projection of the highest stage of the animus, the "wise guide to spiritual truth"[5]:

> Finally ... the animus is the incarnation of meaning. On this highest level he becomes (like the anima) the mediator of the religious experience whereby life acquires a new meaning. He gives the woman spiritual firmness, an invisible inner support that compensates for her outer softness.[6]

And this inner support offered by the animus is most beautifully imaged in the words the male figure speaks to the dreamer, in which he is the fellow laborer, the father, and the lover:

> "From tomorrow I will share everything with you. If you have to work I will share it. If the child cries in the night I will deal with it, and if you need love I will give you love."

The Navel of God

The animus can give tenderness and strength, and also the inner clarity necessary for psychological work. The spiritual function of the animus is further portrayed in the following dream, in which it is through sexual union with a monk that the dreamer, a woman, is shown a spiritual dimension which she terms the "Navel of God," symbolizing a state of total dependence upon Him.

> I am traveling with a monk, an unknown woman, and another monk. We have traveled a long way. Then the scene changes and also the intensity of the dream, which becomes more real than real life. I am in the monk's cell (somehow the other woman and monk have been absorbed into the background of the dream and are not visible). The room is very small, the ground is brown-red (a feeling of warmth). There is a simple pelisse on the floor and the monk and myself are lying on it, naked, embracing each other. I'm as white as the moon and he is slightly golden compared to me. The brown robe of the monk is hanging on a hook on the wall; otherwise the walls are bare. There is a deep sense of intimacy between us and also around us. I feel contained and supported.
>
> I am an explorer and a "God given person." This is my name in the dream, and whatever act I perform with the monk will enhance this quality in me, the "God given person."
>
> While we are making love my attention at one point moves to the area of his navel and belly. It is like absorbing and making a deep contact with that part of him, so I kiss and put my head there, and it is something so sacred and terribly important for me. Suddenly I move my

head and remember something I had dreamt before, and I say to him, "I dreamt of the place that is the Navel of God and I need to go there."

The monk says to me, "I know that place and I will take you there." Then he moves his hand and the place, "the Navel of God," is in front of us like a vision in the room. It is a barren area of yellow color, sloping between two high, grey mountains. The sun is scorching, there is no vegetation. The vision is very powerful, almost dramatic, and I ask the monk what dress I will take to get there. I know I will have pink underwear but I have only an old Indian black dress. I have nothing else and I am frightened that the black color will absorb even more heat from the sun. The monk smiles and he says, "It doesn't matter. It will be terribly hot, but just enough that you can bear it." I know that there will be a lot of wind as well before the scorching sun; and this whole vision powerfully contrasts with the intimacy of the monk's cell. I look at the naked body of my companion with love and admiration. I know that his body is the map to find the Navel of God. Through his body we will find the place.

This profound dream begins with an image of the *quaternio*, two men and two women, who have been traveling a long way together. The *quaternio* is a symbol of psychological wholeness: therefore the four travelers suggest that the dreamer has already reached a certain degree of integration, preparing her for the union that is to take place.

But after this image the intensity of the dream changes and becomes "more real than real life," which often happens in dreams when one encounters the numinous and sacred aspect of oneself. The dream is describing something of great significance for the dreamer, more important, more "real" than her everyday life. She finds herself alone with the monk, with this spiritual aspect of her animus that will lead her away from the world and towards God. The monk's cell, being "very, very small," images this inner rather than outer orientation, and also reflects the dreamer's outer-life situation, which had an ascetic quality as she was totally committed to her analysis and training as a therapist as well as her meditation.

The monk's cell also carries the symbolism of the "well-sealed vessel," the container necessary for inner transformation. At this stage in her inner journey and her outer life the dreamer had decided not to let any external psychological influences, such as might come from a relationship, interfere with her inner work. Relationships and the projections involved give us ample opportunity to contact our own projections and get hold of the *prima materia*. But at times there is also a need to withdraw within oneself in order to work upon the contents of one's own psyche, the alchemical stage of "brooding."

The hermetic vessel is a place of transformation, and in the dream this is imaged first by her making love with the monk, her animus, and then by the visionary landscape, the Navel of God, revealed through him. The union of the couple takes place on the floor of the cell, and their naked bodies give it an archetypal quality, for she is "white as the moon" while he is "slightly golden," suggestive of the sun. They symbolically enact the *coniunctio*, the mystic union of masculine and feminine principles within the psyche, which is often depicted as the marriage of the sun and moon. The alchemists describe the *coniunctio* not only as a chemical combination, but also as a marriage or love affair in which opposing "natures" "embrace one another."[7] The dreamer's feeling of being "contained and supported" echoes the "spiritual firmness and support" that Marie-Louise von Franz describes as an important quality of the animus, a quality that is experienced through this inner union.

The dreamer then describes herself as an "explorer," as the integration of the positive, spiritual aspect of the animus gives her the strength, resolution, and focus necessary to explore the inner world. In previous ages explorers charted unknown lands; today the realm of the psyche is still largely uncharted. Exploring the inner world is a commitment to discover both the light and the darkness, the beauty and the terror, hidden within us.

But as well as an explorer, she is also a "God given person," which is her name in the dream. To be given a name in a dream is of great significance, and this name not only points to the spiritual nature of her quest, but also suggests that everything which comes to the dreamer is a gift from God. To realize that everything we are given comes from the Beloved is to walk the path of purification and poverty, the poverty of being totally dependent upon Him whom we love. This is reflected in the only clothing she has for this journey, "an old, black Indian dress." Black is both the color of the feminine and the color of spiritual poverty, "the poverty of the heart" in which one looks towards God, knowing that He alone can answer our deepest needs. Often we have such a garment hidden within us, waiting for the right time to be worn, the time when we turn away from the outer world and pick up the thread of our spiritual destiny, a thread woven into the fabric of our soul. The dreamer's "old, black Indian dress" is all the dreamer needs to cross the desert to "the Navel of God," the place of being nourished by Him alone. She knows that the journey will be hot, and is frightened that her dress will absorb the heat of the sun, the fire of purification, but we are never asked to bear more than we are able. The monk tells her, "It will be terribly hot, but just enough that you can bear it."

The dreamer's embrace with the monk has awakened her memory of the "Navel of God," a place that belongs to a dream she now must live. Spiritual awakening is the remembrance of a dream that belongs to the soul, a dream of belonging totally to God. But significantly this dream, this memory, is awakened by a physical embrace, a "deep contact" with her animus. She kisses the navel of the monk and puts her head there, and through his navel remembers the Navel of God. However incongruous it might seem that a spiritual quest is furthered through making love to a monk, particularly with reference to the dreamer's own Catholic background, her unconscious tells her "whatever act I perform with the monk will enhance this quality in me, 'the God given person.'" Their embrace is a sacred act that will take her closer to her own divine nature, and at the end of the dream she says, "I know his body is the map to find the Navel of God. Through his body we will find the place." This points to the importance of her including the body in the spiritual process.

The relationship between body and spirit within a woman's psyche is very different from that within a man. For, while masculine consciousness, seeking to free itself from the Great Mother, attempts to separate spirit from matter, within the consciousness of a woman these two "opposites" are experienced as an integral part of one another:

> She understands, symbolically speaking, not with the head but with the whole body, in that her spiritual and corporeal processes are bound together in a way quite foreign to the average man.[8]

The importance the dreamer attaches to the physical body of the monk and the way that the "Navel of God" is reached through his navel reflect the feminine process by which the "spiritual" is realized "within the body." As another woman was told in a dream, "God becomes conscious in the body."

The feminine principle itself is closely related to the world of matter: "Since time immemorial the feminine principle has stood for nature and matter—*Mater Natura*."[9] Just as the woman gives birth and nourishes her children, so does the earth. From Mother Earth are born all living creatures, and with her body she feeds them. They drink from her streams and eat the food she provides.

Because the archetypal feminine is so closely bonded with the earth, a woman's experience of her own feminine self will include the physical. In ancient matriarchal societies this integration of body and spirit was a part of the religious culture, embodied in the figure of the "sacred prostitute," for whom sexuality and spirituality were undivided. However, this attitude, which celebrated an essential part of the feminine, was repressed by the patriarchy, and in Christianity only the body of Christ is sacred. The Catechism asks us to renounce the "sinful lusts of the flesh,"[10] and Saint Paul writes: "Make no provision for the flesh, to fulfil the lusts thereof."[11] As a result, the body and indeed the feminine principle herself have been rejected, repressed, and ultimately identified with evil. The alchemists, in their search for the light hidden in the depths of matter, sought to redress this imbalance, and today any quest for wholeness needs to embrace the physical. This is true for both men and women, but particularly so for women because in their very substance there is this sacred bonding of earth and spirit.

This dream emphasizes the inclusion of the physical dimension. Possibly this is a compensation for the Catholic conditioning of the dreamer; but at the same time as revaluing the feminine world of matter, the dream also stresses that spiritual life is a love affair that involves the whole human being, and even affects the very cells of the body. In mystical experiences of being embraced by the Beloved, everything is included:

> In the night, for instance, one is resting in God—body, mind, everything. The body is included—this is an important point; it too is resting in Him, and this gives such an experience of pure physical bliss. It is like relaxing within the endlessness of love.[12]

From the embrace of the monk the dreamer is taken to the "Navel of God," a landscape of scorching sun and no vegetation. This burning, empty land is a state of total dependence in which one is fully nourished by God. The phrase "Navel of God" also evokes the association of the "World Navel,"

> the symbol of the continuous creation: the mystery of the maintenance of the world through that continuous miracle of vivification which wells within all things.[13]

The "World Navel" is the symbolic place in the world which is "the source of all existence." And while the origin of all nourishment is the same one God, the difference between the "World Navel" and the "Navel of God" is that the former concerns life in this world, the abundance of the harvest, the hearth in the home, while the latter reflects a spiritual orientation in which the seeker looks only to God. Thus the dream embraces the physical in the form of the body of the monk and also images an attitude of spiritual renunciation.

Spiritual poverty is not to deny the beauty and wonder of His creation, but to acknowledge that the creation belongs to the Creator, which means to live in the presence of God. Whatever your outward activity, inwardly you are with Him, and nothing else matters. In his invaluable little book, *The Practice of the Presence of God,* Brother Lawrence describes such a state. Whatever Brother Lawrence did, he did with God: he peeled the potatoes with God, he cooked with God. Throughout his daily work, amid the noise and the clatter of the monastery kitchens, he remained always in an inner attitude of prayer, always in His presence.

If one's inner attention is turned towards God, then the secret beauty of creation reveals itself. The wonder of a woman is that she contains this beauty in her body, because as a part of the Great Mother she embraces the feminine principle of life, the beauty of the Creator made manifest. To be nourished by God is also to acknowledge the wonder of life, its passion and purpose, to see His hidden face reflected, for

> The world is no more than the Beloved's single face;
> In the desire of the One to know its own beauty, we exist.[14]

A mystic can feel the union of the two worlds in the sacredness of her own body, and honor His presence within His own world. To know the "Navel of God" is to know life's deepest connection with its Creator, how the world is just a manifestation of the beauty and wonder of His love.

In the scorching sun of this inner landscape the dreamer will come to know her own connection with Him whom her heart loves. But first she must be burnt by the scorching sun, which will burn away all her attachments to this world, leaving her empty:

> When does Gold Ore become pure Gold? When it is put through a process of fire. So the human being during the training becomes as pure as Gold through suffering. It is the burning away of the dross. I told you that Suffering has a great redeeming quality. Like a drop of water falling on the desert sand is sucked up immediately, so we have to be: nothing and nowhere ... we must disappear.[15]

Only when we have been made empty are we able to realize our true nature which carries the imprint of our Beloved.

For a woman her inner partner is an important figure on this quest. He provides the focus and discrimination necessary for working with the contents of the unconscious. Her masculine consciousness creates the container, the inner boundaries that form the alchemical vessel. Without a positive relationship to the masculine she cannot separate out what belongs to her and what belongs to others, what is to be accepted and integrated and what is to be left outside the vessel of transformation. Without this masculine container her psychic energies remain dispersed, and no real transformation takes place. The masculine also gives her the support and perseverance necessary for this most difficult task, and counters the natural inertia of the feminine, the pull of the Great Mother back into unconsciousness.

But what is essential is that the masculine remains *in service to the feminine*, like the Arthurian knights who were always in service to Our Lady. The woman must remain a "virgin," true to her feminine self, and never prostitute herself to the masculine. This is a great danger in our patriarchal culture, in which women have been conditioned to be frightened of their own nature. If a woman allows her feminine self to be in service to the masculine, then the inner lover becomes a rapist, and the sword of discrimination becomes a murderer's knife, cutting her off from her own instinctual wholeness. How many women have experienced their inner masculine as a rational voice arguing against her innate knowledge, or as a threatening figure chasing her in a dream, wielding this same cutting knife?

Work on the shadow, on both a personal and a collective level, reveals the positive masculine, the lover and friend, who adds the strength and clarity of consciousness to her "diffuse awareness." He helps her to consciously know her instinctual nature, the pure gold of her feminine self. Once she has realized the wonder and beauty of her own nature, the masculine then enables her to live this essence in her outer life, to bring her sacred knowledge of life's wholeness into the world. Without a positive inner partner, her instinctual knowing remains in the unconscious, an unlived dream. Once our dreamer has discovered herself as a "God given person," she needs to live this new-found sense of self, which is her own innermost connection with God. This connection needs to be lived in every cell of her body; only then will its wonder be realized, only then will she fully come to know her own sacred being—the mystery of the feminine side of God made manifest.

THE INNER FEMININE & HER DUAL NATURE

Who is she that looketh forth as the morning, fair as the moon, clear as the sun and terrible as an army with banners?

The Song of Songs[1]

THE DIVINE LOVER

The divine lover appears within us and leads us towards union. Within a woman, as we have seen, this lover takes the form of her own inner masculine self, her animus. He gives her the power and strength she needs to walk through the burning fire that is the path of love. Within the psyche of a man the same lover appears as a woman, veiled and mysterious. Alluring and fascinating, she beckons him into the beautiful and terrible depths of his own being.

The anima arises like Venus from the waters of the unconscious. She has many forms; she is both virgin and temptress. For many men she is their most powerful archetypal figure, and every romantic poem or song is written in homage to her. From the first time you see her you know that "you have always been her lover." Like Ariadne she holds the thread that can guide a man through the labyrinthine maze of his unconscious, back to the hidden core of his being. She carries the image of a man's soul, of his own inner mystery. It is through union with her that the Christ Child, the Self, is born. In much Sufi poetry the anima echoes the Beloved; in the images of a woman's beauty a divine beauty is mirrored:

I became love-crazed when my Beloved
  like the new moon, revealed an eyebrow,
    displayed herself, then closed the door.[2]

La Belle Dame Sans Merci

The feminine is both creative and destructive, nurtures life and yet also devours it. The anima has her dark side. She is the siren who lures men into the waters of the psyche and leaves them there to drown. Belonging to the impersonal depths, she is cold and uncaring; she seeks only power and uses all her magical attraction to imprison consciousness. Keats personifies her as "La Belle Dame sans Merci." He describes how a brave knight-at-arms is captivated by her beauty, her long hair and wild eyes, how she sings him "a faery's song" and feeds him "honey wild, and manna dew, And sure in language strange she said—'I love thee true.'" But once she has seduced him, she leaves him; and in a dream he sees all those whom she has enchanted and left desolate:

I saw pale kings and princes too,
  Pale warriors, death-pale were they all;
They cried—"La Belle Dame sans Merci
  Hath thee in thrall!"
I saw their starved lips in the gloam,
  With horrid warning gaped wide,
And I awoke and found me here,
  On the cold hill's side.[3]

The same archetypal story is told in the film *The Blue Angel.* Marlene Dietrich plays the anima figure, an actress in a small touring theater which visits a provincial town where the well-respected school teacher watches a performance and becomes entranced by her. He leaves his job and joins the theater company in order to be with her. She totally degrades him, making him act the part of the clown. Finally the theater returns to his home town and she forces him to play the clown before his former pupils and fellow citizens. Unable to endure such humiliation, he goes to his former classroom and hangs himself. As in Keats's poem, the anima has woven her spell, seducing and then destroying her victim.

The *femme fatale* is an inner figure as much as an alluring outer woman, and many men have been caught by her cold passion. They are often unable to relate to women but are fed only by fantasies which leave them starving. One friend who had great difficulty forming a relationship with a woman had a dream in which he was shown the effigy of a witch, under which was written "she can put out any fire." She is the enemy of consciousness and warmth of feeling. Like the spider mother, she is an aspect of the devouring feminine which is merciless and cruel. She alienates those whom she has bitten, leaving them isolated, and, in the words of Keats's poem, "alone and palely loitering."

THE VIRGIN AND THE DRAGON

The power of the anima derives from the archetypal world, for she stands between the personal and the collective unconscious, her image merging back into the Great Mother herself. In her darkest form she is Medusa, whose glance has the power to petrify. Fascinated and yet frightened, man has projected the dark anima onto both the *femme fatale* and the witch. Just before writing this passage I saw a car sticker which read "My ex-wife's car is a broomstick." This "joke" points to the depths of fear a man can have about the dark woman who haunts his dreams, and many innocent women have been tortured and burned as witches because of this fear. Unable to face the darkness within, he has persecuted his projection.

Man's fear of the dark feminine derives from his fear of the Great Mother, the dragon mother, who represents the deepest powers of the unconscious. Hers is a realm in which there is no light of consciousness. In this primal place there is no morality, no division into light or darkness. It is the instinctual jungle world—"red in tooth and claw"—and the domain of the tiger who symbolizes the undifferentiated energy of the goddess.

This fear of the feminine is very real and should not be dismissed. Towards the end of his life Jung said, "Woman is a very, very strong being, magical. That's why I am afraid of women."[4] If we are to make a creative relationship with the inner feminine we must acknowledge this fear. In myths a virgin, symbol of the anima, is often held captive by a dragon. In previous ages the heroic quest involved slaying the dragon. Man needed to free himself from his instinctual drives and the fearsome power of the Great Mother. Only then could he find the anima, his individual feminine self. While the anima is an archetypal figure, with her roots in the collective unconscious, she also symbolizes a personal relationship to the feminine. A man's anima figure is very personal and intimate, unlike his relationship with the mother in which his individuality is easily lost in the collective nature of the mother archetype.

A man's relationship with the feminine is first held in the grip of the dragon, the Great Mother archetype. A man who remains so imprisoned always looks for a mother figure—for him all women are identified with the mother. In this state there can be no individual creative relationship with the unconscious. In order to realize his own individual relationship to the inner and outer feminine, he must free the virgin, his own pure feminine self.

But in our era, too many dragons have been slain, and we now need the power of the Great Mother to heal ourselves and our world. The anima still needs to be set free, but the dragon needs to be accepted, not killed. We need to look at our fear of the feminine and in the mirror of consciousness see her darkest face. Only then will we cease to project this fear; only then will we integrate rather than reject the powerful energies of the feminine.

The anima often first appears in her idealized form. She is a pure and beautiful virgin. In our Western culture we have separated the light and the dark aspects of the feminine. The heroic ideal honored "Mary, Queen of Heaven" and rejected and repressed her darker, earthier twin. This twin first appeared in the Judeo-Christian tradition as Lilith, the first wife of Adam, who refused to be subservient to him. In killing the dragon we may have freed a virgin but we have rejected the instinctual power of the feminine. The feminine is as much the dragon as the virgin and we can no longer afford to separate the two. We need the primal power of the instinctual world. If we look at the face of the dragon with love and the reflective quality of consciousness, its energy can be integrated. This is a work as much for women as for men, for women need to accept their own primal power as much as men need to integrate this feminine potential. Here lies the heroic quest of our age, for the child of the future needs to ride on the back of the dragon.

In descending into the unconscious, we meet this natural energy of the feminine, which the romantic, idealized image of the anima is unable to contain. We see this idealized image represented in Shakespeare's *Hamlet*, in the prince's initial love for Ophelia. She is "the celestial and my soul's idol, the most beautiful Ophelia"; no earthly images intrude upon his vision. But like the moon, the feminine has a dark side which cannot be ignored forever: "The baying of Hecate is always there, whether it sound from near or from far."[5] Hamlet's destiny forces him to confront the dark side of the feminine in his mother's instinctual sexuality, her adulterous affair with his uncle Claudius. In disgust he accuses her of bestial sexuality:

> Nay, but to live
> In the rank sweat of an enseamed bed,
> Stew'd in corruption, honeying and making love
> Over the nasty sty![6]

Yet what this image evokes is not merely animal squalor, but associations with the Great Mother. In ancient times honey was sacred to the Earth Goddess, and the "nasty sty" relates to the pig which symbolizes the creative female, "the fruitful and receptive womb." Both honey and the pig were associated with the female genitals: there is a Hindu marriage custom of daubing the woman's genitals with honey, and "the most primitive and ancient of the pig associations is with the female genitals, which even in Greek and Latin were called 'pig.'"[7]

Sexuality and fertility belong to the domain of the Great Mother. Here Shakespeare images both her sensuality and her amoral, instinctual nature. Hamlet's Ophelia, his "soul's idol," cannot embrace this deeper and darker anima, and so she dissolves back into the unconscious, first into madness and then drowned in the "glassy stream." Later Hamlet is able to integrate both poles of the feminine, and so realize its transcendent nature. When Ophelia has been buried, Gertrude describes this state of inner peace that follows the "madness" of Hamlet's descent into the unconscious:

> Anon, as patient as the female dove
> When that her golden couplets are disclos'd,
> His silence will sit drooping.[8]

Here the "female dove" corresponds to the feminine spirit of God, the highest form of the feminine.[9] This is the transformation of the feminine archetype, whose dual aspects are recognized as the "golden couplets." In the inner alchemical process the conflict of opposites has become pure gold.

A Seductive and Cunning Lady

The negative aspect of the anima takes on many forms and she does not always appear projected onto an external figure. The anima is the mediator between the conscious mind and the unconscious and thus through her a man has access to the creative energies of the unconscious. She is his muse but in her negative form she does not allow a man to taste the fruits of his creativity. She would keep his potential trapped in the unconscious or, as in the case of some great artists like van Gogh or Wagner, she so overwhelms him with the creative power of the unconscious that his own individual consciousness is lost in insanity.

Jung experienced this aspect of the feminine as an invisible presence full of deep cunning. When he was working with the fantasies of the unconscious, an inner voice told him it was "art," and he realized that if he believed her

> she might then easily have seduced me into believing that I was a misunderstood artist, and that my so-called artistic nature gave me the right to neglect reality.[10]

The dark side of the anima always tries to lure us away from reality into the fascinating but murky waters of the unconscious. Our defense against her is the power of consciousness, which keeps us grounded in the ordinary, everyday world while at the same time facilitating a bridge into the inner world. Jung stresses the dangers of the anima and the importance of consciously working with the contents of the unconscious:

> The insinuations of the anima, the mouthpiece of the unconscious, can utterly destroy a man. In the final analysis the decisive factor is consciousness, which can understand the manifestations of the unconscious and take up a position towards them.[11]

One friend, whose work, like Jung's, involved both factual research and working creatively with the unconscious, experienced this dark lady as a fascinating sequence of ideas that suddenly came to him and appeared to distract him from the main direction of his writing. For a while he deliberated as to whether to follow these ideas or to stick to his previous direction. He was aware of their fascination and of the inherent danger of being lured away from the central theme of his work; yet, at the same time, he consciously chose to follow up these new ideas. The importance of making this decision *consciously* can not be overestimated, for it meant that he had not been seduced by the unconscious. It had a profound psychological effect as was shown in a dream he had soon after. This dream has the quality of a myth or fairy tale:

> I am involved with others in a war against an evil man and his woman. Our base and stronghold is a strange building like the upper half of a huge, lichen-covered crab shell. It's perfectly round and symmetrical and has about ten or twelve entrances arranged regularly all around it. It seems impenetrable. I am the leader in the war, but I'm also totally dissociated from the leader—whom I can watch and observe as a distinct person.
>
> The evil man's woman hatches a ploy. She takes on a human form—the form of a physically beautiful, sensuous, lightly clothed woman—and she enters the stronghold in human disguise. I, the leader, see through her disguise. I know exactly who she is but I consciously decide to play along with her disguise—hiding what I know just as she is hiding who she is—and I deliberately seduce and make love to her.
>
> The next morning the other people in the stronghold come up to us as we lie in my bed. We are not in a separate bedroom but next to

one of the arches in the single vast room that makes up the stronghold. She gets out of the bed and as she does so, young and attractive as she was, in front of everybody's eyes she starts changing rapidly—second by second—into an old, senile, dying woman. I, the leader and hero, remain lying on the bed, dying of a disease which I caught through making love to her. This is what she meant to do, and her seduction ploy has succeeded. But, as I am dying on the bed, the celestial voice of a woman speaks out clearly and loudly as if from a loudspeaker which reverberates throughout the building: "If you write a book which you owe (no matter why) to someone else, you cannot yourself write books."

I have heard that voice before and I know who she is. Only once in my life has she spoken to me, when I was lying on my bed fifteen years ago, and what she said then changed my life.

This dream begins with a war, symbolic of an inner conflict, between the dreamer's ego and his shadow, "an evil man," and the dark side of his anima. As frequently happens, the shadow and the negative anima are in league: she is the evil man's woman. Furthermore, the dreamer's stronghold seems impenetrable. It cannot be defeated by a direct attack from the shadow. Direct confrontation can often be defeated by reason, but the anima's power of "insinuation" and "suggestion" can, as Jung warns, be far more dangerous. Her "ploys" can undermine a man's consciousness, devalue what he is doing, misdirect his attention—often without his even being aware of what is happening. (In contrast the negative animus will often attack directly with well-reasoned arguments: "Nobody will want to read the book you are writing," or "Can't you see you are a total failure? You are unable to relate properly to a man.")[12]

However, at the beginning of this dream, the dreamer's ego, which is the "leader in the war," is also "totally dissociated from the leader—whom I can watch and observe as a distinct person." The importance of such an attitude of detachment, or "observing," is that it "counterbalances the devouring powers of the unconscious." It is this attitude which enables the dreamer to experience the dark side of the anima without becoming lost in her seductive embrace.

The anima is the mistress of disguise, and in this dream, as in many fairy tales, the evil witch-like woman takes on the guise of a beautiful, sensuous woman to beguile the hero. However, the conscious detachment of the dreamer enables him to see through her disguise, though he allows himself to play along with it. In the real-life dynamic he was aware of the dangerous fascination of the ideas that had come from the unconscious, but decided to work with them. Playing a perilous role, he "deliberately seduced and made love to" the evil man's woman.

To make love is symbolic of integration; through accepting the deceitful nature of the dark aspect of the anima, the dreamer was able to consciously experience and thus integrate her negative energy. When these lovers awake the next morning, the other people in the stronghold come up to them, which also suggests an integration (as aspects of the psyche come together). Furthermore the lovers are not in a separate bedroom, but "next to one of the arches in the single vast room that makes up the stronghold." The dreamer's psyche is thus imaged as a single inner space without the experience of separation. The arch also carries an auspicious symbolism, for to pass under an arch in initiation ceremonies symbolizes "being reborn, leaving behind the old nature."[13]

The integration of the dark aspect of the anima is a profound initiation, but first the dreamer must experience the stage of putrefaction, decay and death, as the old attitudes of consciousness break down. The beautiful, seductive woman becomes an old and senile woman. This is an image found in many fairy tales, as the negative anima loses her powers to bewitch and is shown in her true form as an old witch. But this woman is not only senile, but dying, and so is the dreamer, dying of a "disease ... caught through making love to her." This is what the woman had intended; she had meant to destroy him, to lure him into the unconscious where his consciousness would be lost forever. But, because of his conscious acceptance, this death will not leave him lost in the unconscious; rather it will lead to a transformation of consciousness. In particular, his old attitude towards the feminine and his relationship with her creative potential will die so that a new relationship can be born. The negative anima has been transformed into Sophia, the divine aspect of the feminine, the figure of wisdom. Hers is the voice he now hears speaking out. Purified of her distorting, negative aspect, the highest form of the feminine can now be heard clearly through his whole psyche.

The dreamer has heard Sophia's voice once, fifteen years before, and it changed his life. He has never forgotten it, and now, through integrating the dark side of the anima, he will be able to have a direct relationship with Sophia. She will guide him in his work, but first she tells him what must be a basic principle for his work: "If you write a book which you owe (no matter why) to someone else, you cannot yourself write books." This may appear to be just a simple precept, "to thine owne self be true," but it has a profound psychological significance. In working with the creative potential of the anima we are channeling energy from within. If we are not true to our deepest self, then this energy can become distorted. If this energy from the unconscious is distorted, it can corrupt and become very destructive.

Our only motive in working with the energy of the unconscious should be to serve our deepest creative purpose; this purpose is always in harmony with our true inner self. If the individual is not free to follow his own inner guidance, if this creative energy is used to serve any other purpose (if the book is owed, for whatever reason, to someone else), this energy will become contaminated and will contaminate. This applies to any allegiance to an external cause or ideal, because however justified a cause may be, it imprisons the individual within a certain conscious framework. The most dangerous case is when this energy is used for the power purposes of the ego, for the sake of personal gain or prestige. This primordial energy is numinous, dynamic, but essentially amoral. It has no quality of discrimination, and will feed the power-hungry shadow, which in time will become strong enough to dominate the ego.

Before the full potential of the unconscious can be used creatively, the shadow must be confronted and the dark side of the anima unmasked. We need a pure vessel to contain these powerful forces. It is for this reason that the deeper we go into the unconscious and the more we channel its energy, the higher is the ethical standard which is required. It is not that we need to be a morally "better person," but that our consciousness needs to be pure enough not to be corrupted or distorted by the primal energies from within.

Behind the Dance of Illusion

The anima is a temptress, deceiving a man not only with the bewitching nature of the unconscious, but also with the myriad attractions of the outer world. She is the mistress of illusion; hers is the dance of *maya*. Jung describes *maya* as an aspect of the anima:

> She is the great illusionist, the seductress who draws him [man] into life with her Maya—and not only into life's reasonable and useful aspects, but into its frightful paradoxes and ambivalences where good and evil, success and ruin, hope and despair counterbalance one another.[14]

As Salome she is the temptress, keeping man entranced in the beauty of this world, hiding her real purpose behind a seductive veil. The ascetics who turn their eyes from women and punish their flesh try to escape her power. But only too often this temptress is merely repressed, and she exerts her fascination through the shadow. She becomes a demon who haunts the dreams of the pious.

But once a man has confronted her dark, seductive nature and is no longer in her grip, then the feminine reveals her higher nature as Sophia. Sophia carries the deep wisdom of the soul, and allows us to see through the veils of the illusion and glimpse the real beauty that lies behind. She enables us to see the secret face of creation. Sufi poetry speaks of the beauty of the human form because it is a reflection of the formless. The form of woman holds the highest essence because she is the most beautiful creation of the Great Artist. According to Ibn 'Arabî, "Woman is the highest form of earthly beauty, but earthly beauty is nothing unless it is a manifestation and reflection of the Divine Qualities."[15] Thus, in Sufi poetry, each of her features has symbolic significance representing qualities of the Eternal Beloved. The eye symbolizes the quality of the mystery of God's vision; the mole or beauty spot signifies the Divine Essence itself; the twist or curve of her curl is a metaphor for Divine mysteries:[16]

> By the fragrant breeze from your tresses' ringlet
> I am forever drunk;
> While the devastating guile of your bewitching eyes
> devastates me at every breath.[17]

The eternal beauty seen projected in the wonder of romantic love is a glimpse of our own eternal nature. Sophia draws aside the veils of the dancer, and allows us to wonder at the divine beauty of the feminine side of God. He for whom we long comes to us in so many guises, and with the wisdom of the feminine we are able to recognize Him in His creation, hear the music that is beneath life's surface, and see the true beauty in everyday life. I was once on an airline flight with my teacher, and looking down the aisle saw a heavily made-up stewardess walk towards me. I have always been prejudiced against women wearing a lot of make-up, particularly when it is an attempt to disguise their natural age. But just as this thought came into my mind, my teacher turned to me, and with the simple wisdom of Sophia awoke me, saying, "Human beings are so beautiful, aren't they? Aren't all human beings so beautiful?"

The Secret Places of the Soul

Within the psyche the feminine carries the mystery hidden in the dance of creation. As much as she is a temptress, she is also a guide who, like Dante's Beatrice, can lead a man to the secret places of the soul. Once we have accepted her dark face, she can no longer devour us or lead us astray. She shows us the beauty of our inner self, which is none other than her own face unveiled. This is her role in the following dream:

> I am in a castle and am being taken by an extremely beautiful woman to a part of the castle which is not open to the public. It is a secret place which nobody else is allowed to see. I go in. It is a most wonderfully beautiful room with chandeliers. It contains a huge pool, rectangular like a ballroom. In the middle of the pool there are beautiful water lilies in a mandala-shaped flower arrangement.
>
> The pool is full of the most beautiful fish I have ever seen. They are absolutely extraordinary. They have just been fed and I am able to feed them a little bit. They are a beautiful coral color and are big and fat like those very old goldfish one finds in Japan. There is also a frog there.

> Then I notice that the pool is also full of giraffes. There is one huge giraffe and lots of baby giraffes. They are able to breathe underwater and are perfectly all right there. That is where they lived.
>
> I accompany the woman and she takes me round the castle.

In the castle of the Self this dreamer's beautiful anima takes him to a secret place which is not open to the public and which "nobody else is allowed to see." Living in the world of the ego and the bustle of our daily lives, we rarely enter the secret places of our own innermost being. Sometimes a dream will open a window through which we can glimpse the wonder that we really are. In the public world our beauty is usually veiled, not only to others but to our self. Only when we withdraw—into the silence of meditation or into the deep peace of sleep—is this veil lifted and we see the mystery and smell the fragrance of our bride, who has long been waiting for our embrace:

> A garden inclosed is my sister my spouse; a spring shut up, a fountain sealed.
>
> Thy plants are an orchard of pomegranates with pleasant fruits; camphire with spikenard....
>
> Awake, O north wind; and come, thou south; blow upon my garden, that the spices thereof may flow out. Let my beloved come into his garden and eat his pleasant fruits.[18]

The feminine takes us into her garden, a place rich with the fruits and the flowers of the soul. The longing to find this "secret garden" is deeper than sexual attraction; the garden is filled with the wisdom that belongs to the heart. This is the real meeting place of lovers; in the fleeting moments of sexual bliss we taste its fruit. Sexual ecstasy is a momentary experience of the bliss that lies within the heart, given to us for the sake of procreation. According to Irina Tweedie it is "really the soul and not the body that is the experiencer."[19] If a couple make love with both their souls and their bodies, and in the moment of bliss give everything as an offering to the One True Lover, they can then enter this fragrant garden that is the ecstatic home of the mystic. Mystical states can be very erotic (though the energy is not felt in the sex organs but in the throat *chakra*); in these moments of bliss, the mystic is always the receptive one, the lover impregnated by the spirit of the Beloved. Whether man or woman, we become feminine in this experience; and in its ecstasy we are both enslaved and freed, ravished and purified:

> Take mee to you, imprison mee, for I
> Except you enthrall mee, never shall be free,
> Nor ever chast, except you ravish mee.[20]

The mysteries of the soul are feminine. In the beautiful room hidden in the castle of the dreamer all the images are feminine. There is a huge pool in the midst of which there are beautiful water lilies. The lily is a flower sacred to the Virgin Goddess, but it also exhibits the quality of the lotus, for it rises from the mud to flower only when it reaches the surface of the water. Thus the lily images the process of inner transformation, which begins in the muddy depths of the unconscious and only flowers when it finally emerges into consciousness. This is why the ego is unaware of the really important inner changes, and the individual so often feels that nothing is happening. The alchemical processes that change our whole being grow silently in the depths, transforming the structure of our psyche from within. Transformations that are not rooted in this way are rarely lasting; they are merely like waves on the surface. Real inner work requires patience and perseverance; only those who are truly committed will continue to walk along the hard and stony path without experiencing obvious results.

But the flowers have opened and the water lilies form a mandala. The beauty of the Self opens before the eyes of the dreamer, and that beauty is always awe-inspiring, for it brings into consciousness our own divine nature. It reminds us of our real home.

> What a wonderful lotus it is, that blooms at the heart of the spinning wheel of the universe! Only a few pure souls know of its true delight.
>
> Music is all around it, and there the heart partakes of the joy of the Infinite Sea.[21]

The pool is also full of fish, symbolizing the contents of the unconscious which the alchemical process brings together and transforms. But these fish are "the most beautiful fish I had ever seen," for here again the dreamer sees the true beauty of his inner self, hidden in the unconscious. They are "a beautiful coral color." Coral is the tree of the Mother Goddess, and because the inner transformation takes place in the depths, it is under the dominion of the Great Goddess. The Great Mother may resist the evolution of individual consciousness, but the heart is the king and the Self is the master and the "source of every power." Even the Great Goddess follows the will of the Self. Therefore if the seeker—through meditation and aspiration—

focuses on this essence that lives within the heart, the energies of the Goddess will help and not hinder the evolution of the soul. Coral is also suggestive of pink which is the color of love. This hints at an inner secret of the path of love: that it infuses the whole psyche of the seeker with the energy of love. The psyche and all of its contents become permeated from within with the transforming energy of love.

In addition to the fish, there is a frog in the pool. The frog is a lunar symbol of renewal and transformation, emphasizing the feminine potential for inner change. But then the dreamer notices that the pool is also "full of giraffes." With its long eyelashes and gentle ways the giraffe is the most graceful and feminine of creatures. These giraffes are happy underwater, for that's where they live. In the unconscious are the beauty and grace of the feminine. These qualities have a deep wisdom, a wisdom of silence rather than speech. The graceful walk of a woman is movement in harmony with nature; for the Sufi the curve of her eyebrow symbolizes the subtlety of Divine beauty. We have become so conditioned to value only knowledge communicated through words that we have forgotten what is contained in the senses: how touch can evoke hidden qualities of feeling, how a caress can convey understanding. The giraffes image the instinctual world of the feminine which has qualities we have long overlooked, but now need in order to bring warmth into the coldness of our rational existence.

The Messenger of Meaning

The anima can open a man to the music of his soul and thus allow its song to manifest in his life. She is the personification of his creativity, and meeting with her brings its fire flowing from the source of his being. Connecting us with our inner powers, she brings meaning into our everyday world, which each of us manifests in our own unique way. With her hands every act can be an offering of the soul, each gesture creative. Baking bread or writing a song, painting a picture or planting a flower, each can speak of the inner mystery and allow its beauty and meaning to be heard.

Meaning does not come from the external world, but from within, from the archetypal world. The primal, archetypal beings who inhabit it are imprinted with meaning. The archetypes do not have an identifiable meaning; they do not mean something specific in the sense that *bon* in French means "good" in English. They rather have qualities of meaning; they make things meaningful. Huston Smith, the contemporary American philosopher, designates this type of meaning as "existential"; it is "the kind we have in mind when we say that something is meaningful."[22] However, because our language has developed to describe the external world of the senses, it has very few words to describe this type of meaning. We can say that something is "very meaningful" or "quite meaningful," but the different ways in which things feel meaningful cannot be expressed. This is true of our language for feeling as well. In Sanskrit there are ninety-six words to describe love: love for a child is different from love for a brother; a different word expresses a husband's love for his wife from the one that expresses a wife's love for her husband; and the love for a guru is also a different word. In our language there is only one word; the poverty of our feelings is reflected in the poverty of our language. We have not named the different qualities of feeling because we have not valued them. Our rejection of the feminine has caused the qualities of meaning she brings with her to be left out of our lives.

The anima is the messenger of meaning. Embracing the physical and symbolic worlds, she lets us taste the substance of our soul in our day-to-day life. But work with the anima should never be self-indulgent; it should be directed towards a greater understanding of the inner world. This need for a greater understanding was encapsulated in a dream in which the dreamer was about to make love with his anima figure when the teacher appeared at the other end of the room, and, pointing to a symbol on the wall, said to the dreamer, "What does this mean?" The dreamer had to understand the symbolic meaning of his relationship with his anima. This has to be a conscious union, for only then is the meaning of the symbolic inner world infused into the outer world, a place which today has too often become a wasteland.

The highest form of the anima is Sophia, who, personifying the wisdom of the soul, brings the deepest meaning of the Self into our everyday life. In Shakespeare's *King Lear* she is Cordelia, Lear's daughter who refuses to flatter his ego and is banished because of her refusal and her silence. The king then has to confront the dark, power-hungry aspect of the anima in his other daughters, Goneril and Regan. They strip him of his worldly status and leave him destitute on the heath in the storm of his own unconscious. Only then can he find his own inner wisdom, which is so different from that valued by the world. This is the wisdom of the fool, a wisdom well-known to the Sufi. It is the natural wisdom of the Self. When Lear is finally reunited with Cordelia, he no longer cares about the world of the ego, "Who loses and who wins," but looks behind its veil of appearances: he sees his task now as to

> ...take upon's the mystery of things,
> As if we were God's spies.[23]

Sufis are known as "God's spies" for they see into the hearts of people where the real mystery and meaning are hidden. Ibn 'Arabi described Sophia as "an image raising its head from the secrecy of the heart." She connects us with our own divine nature and so allows us to see the inner purpose hidden within everything. Within all of creation is a hidden message reminding us of our real home, for everything—every leaf and stone—sings the song of its creator. Through her ears we can hear this sublime song, through her eyes we can see His face reflected in every sky and every street. Her greatest wisdom is the way that she beckons us into the beyond. In her highest emanation she is the Divine Sophia, the feminine aspect of the Higher Self. Our union with her is a merging into our own mystery:

> Dearly beloved!
> I have called you so often and you have
> not heard me.
> I have shown myself to you so often and
> you have not seen me.
> I have made myself fragrance so often, and
> you have not smelled me,

Savorous food, and you have not tasted me.
Why can you not reach me through the
object you touch
Or breathe me through sweet perfumes?
Why do you not see me? Why do you not
hear me?
Why? Why? Why?

For you my delights surpass all other
delights,
And the pleasure I procure you surpasses
all other pleasures.
For you I am preferable to all other
good things,
I am Beauty, I am Grace.

Love me, love me alone.
Love yourself in me, in me alone.
Attach yourself to me,
No one is more inward than I.
Others love you for their own sakes,
I love you for yourself.
And you, you flee from me.

Dearly beloved!
You cannot treat me fairly,
For if you approach me,
It is because I have approached you.

I am nearer to you than yourself,
Than your soul, than your breath.
Who among creatures
Would treat you as I do?
I am jealous of you over you,

I want you to belong to no other,
Not even to yourself.
Be mine, be for me as you are in me,
Though you are not even aware of it.

Dearly beloved!
Let us go toward Union.
And if we find the road
That leads to separation,
We will destroy separation.
Let us go hand in hand.
Let us enter the presence of Truth.
Let it be our judge
And imprint its seal upon our union
For ever.[24]

THE UNATTAINABLE BRIDE

Thou hast ravished my heart, my sister, my spouse; thou hast ravished my heart with one of thine eyes, with one chain of thy neck.

The Song of Songs[1]

The Princess and Her Slave

In *The Conference of the Birds* 'Attâr tells the story of a princess, as beautiful as the moon, who falls in love with one of her father's slaves. Love takes possession of her and she longs to be with him. Yet she realizes that it will be fatal for both her and her slave if anyone knows that they have enjoyed each other's love. She tells her maids of honor of her sorrowful state, and they devise a plan that will fulfill her desires without anyone knowing, not even the slave himself.

In the evening one of the maids goes to the slave and offers him a drugged cup of wine. He falls asleep and then the maids carry out their plan. They carry him into the chamber of the princess, and when he opens his eyes, still a little drugged, and sees the dazzling splendor of the room and the bewildering beauty of the princess, he thinks he is in paradise and falls into ecstasy. In this state the princess presses sweet kisses on his mouth, and "lost herself in his eyes." He possesses her and they make rapturous love until dawn. Then again a maid of honor gives him a drugged drink, and when he awakes he finds himself again in his quarters.

He finds it impossible to describe what has happened. As if in a dream he has spent the night in rapture with a woman whose beauty only serves to confuse him. Who she is he will never know, but some hidden secret of love has been revealed to him.

In this story, the princess is an image of the Beloved. The Beloved is in love with the slave (a synonym for the Sufi, who is known as a slave of God), for it is the Beloved who is seeking us, calling to us, longing for us. We always think that we are the seeker, but the deeper mystery is that we are called. The seeker is in reality the sought, as it is said in the Qur'an: "He loves them, and they love Him."[2] Rûmî describes how it is always the Beloved who secretly seduces us back into His arms:

> sultan, saint, pickpocket;
> love has everyone by the ear
> dragging us to God
> by secret ways
>
> I never knew
> that God, too, desires us.[3]

When the slave awakens from her embrace, it is as if from a dream, for dreams are the meeting point of the inner and outer worlds. Through our dreams He beckons to us; and how often is falling in love like falling into a dream? Through the process of projection, the Beloved often appears in human form: a woman takes on the splendor and beauty of a goddess, a man the majesty of a god. Sometimes one can see how this projection falls upon another person—see this person both with and without the magical garment that is woven from the fabric of our own unconscious. With this projection the other is infinitely fascinating, unknown and yet strangely familiar. One's inner attention is unconsciously attracted towards this person, and in a crowded room one's eyes will be drawn to him or her as if by an invisible thread. The person seems a part of oneself; this attraction is the attraction of one's own unconscious mystery. Yet it can happen that suddenly the projection is withdrawn, and the other is no longer magical, but just an ordinary human being.

The Beauty of God's Feminine Form

Part of the fascination of the feminine is that she embraces the wonder of creation. The principle of matter itself is feminine and the whole of creation can be seen as God's feminine form. When a man projects the anima onto a woman, what he experiences is a sense of both completion and awe. The beauty of the inner and outer are fused together. The Goddess cannot be worshiped in the abstract because one of her essential qualities is physical manifestation. The animus has different qualities and the masculine spirit has a more abstract nature. A woman can love a man for his intellect, for his spirit, and does not need to see his physical appearance as beautiful. But a man has a need to see his lover's body as beautiful; he seeks Aphrodite. This is why there are so many girlie magazines; they reflect this need—though sadly Aphrodite's sensual beauty has been debased to the level of pornography. Yet woman herself, like the earth, can never be impure:

> The woman is like Gold, she is like the Earth, she is never impure.... Gold, even if it falls into the latrine and is taken out and is cleaned, it is

> the same, and its value is not less. The Earth purifies everything—the changing seasons ... the earth is always pure.[4]

A woman's body and her sexuality are a part of the sacred substance of the earth. In the following dream an anima figure embraces all these aspects of the feminine, expressing how within a man's psyche she carries this precious gold:

> Half-naked I meet Aurelia, a former girl friend of mine. Suddenly I am aware that she too is half-naked. She is wearing a tunic, open at the sides so that I can see her marvelous modeled body. Her muscles are strong; she reminds me of Diana.
>
> We start playfully to try and catch each other and within a moment we are out in nature. We run across a freshly ploughed field of rich brown soil. The ground curves up to a small hill, and Aurelia is nearly ten meters away from me, lying stretched out on her back on the bare ground.
>
> Half-flying I jump towards her, landing very softly on her belly so that I directly touch her vulva. Suddenly I realize that her belly and the area between her legs are covered with crumbled earth. I put my hands into the soil, feeling how precious the earth is. Then, as in a holy ceremony, Aurelia takes me very softly and leads me into her body.

The dreamer's anima figure is named Aurelia, which is a derivative of *aurum* (gold in Latin). Seeing her "marvelous modeled body," the dreamer associates her with Diana, the Roman equivalent of Artemis, the archetype of a pure, primitive femininity. Diana is a woodland goddess, a huntress who belongs to the natural world. It is not within doors or upon a bed that the dreamer embraces this archetypal figure, but upon the "rich brown soil." Her sexuality and the earth are interrelated, and through her the dreamer realizes how "precious the earth is." Her gold is the gold of his own natural feminine self. And at the end of the dream she leads him "into her body," initiating him into the sacred mystery of the feminine. Here the dream's imagery echoes the ancient song of the goddess Inanna, the oldest of the goddesses of passion, love, and death:

> My vulva, the horn,
> The Boat of Heaven,
> Is full of eagerness like the young moon.
> My untilled land lies fallow.
>
> As for me, Inanna,
> Who will plow my vulva?
> Who will plow my high field?
> Who will plow my wet ground?
>
> Dumuzi answers:
>
> Great Lady, the king will plow your vulva.
> I, Dumuzi the King, will plow your vulva.
>
> To which Inanna responds:
>
> Then plow my vulva, man of my heart!
> Plow my vulva![5]

The earth and sexuality are a part of the ancient feminine rites of fertility. The dreamer has been initiated into this ritual and from now on his relationship with the feminine will be transformed. He has experienced both the beauty and the holiness of her natural energy. In ancient times the sacred prostitute performed this function of initiation in the temples of the Goddess. Those times are past and her temples have long been destroyed or crumbled into dust. But, under the guidance of the anima, the same sacred process can take place within the psyche of a man. Indeed the anima offers a more direct inner experience, a closer connection with the Goddess. While the priestess was a vessel of the Goddess, the anima is herself an archetypal figure. She is the Goddess clothed in a man's own personal imagery.

The anima, who can initiate a man into the mystery of his own feminine being, is projected onto a woman who is able to embody, however fleetingly, the feminine's fascination and beauty. Yet a woman who attracts an anima projection does not have to be physically beautiful. Cleopatra, one of the great anima figures, is not supposed to have been physically attractive.[6] But a man has a need to experience a woman's body as beautiful, to both see and touch Aphrodite's physical form. Beauty is in the eye of the beholder, and through the magic of projection any woman can appear sublime.

There has been much misunderstanding of the archetypal origin of this need, and in recent years many women have rebelled against feeling that they are appreciated only for their bodies. Earlier I discussed a woman's dream in which she was the king's mistress, and "just an object" for him to look at. Yet it is important to see the difference between a man's need to experience a woman's body as a way of contacting the Goddess, and the soulless objectification of women that patriarchal culture has fostered by destroying the inner temples of the feminine and seeking to possess her outer form as an object. A man's anima projection onto a woman can be a way for him to reinstate the feminine both within and outside himself, to honor her in all her forms. As the highest form of earthly beauty, a woman can bring a man into contact with something he can never possess but can treasure within his heart:

> The bird is beyond seeking, yet it is most clearly visible. The Formless is in the midst of all forms. I sing the glory of forms.[7]

But only too often when the anima is projected onto a woman she feels that she has been made an object, an image rather than a person. She feels that she is not seen for herself and may try to break or escape from the projection. Could this be because we do not know what to do with this image of divinity and so confuse it with the personal? If a woman can see herself as a priestess of the divine Feminine, can the projection then be honored in its own place? Is it possible that the projection is then not a prison but a shrine, a process through which she can see beyond the personal into the archetypal world? Through her lover's projection can she connect with her own inner divinity, the same divinity that is the source of his attraction?

UNCONDITIONAL LOVE

Because our culture has rejected the numinous, we do not know what to do with this energy when it appears. For most people the experience of falling in love is the most direct and powerful archetypal experience they have; but the sacred schools that taught people how to integrate the archetypal world have long been destroyed. We have to learn anew how to make the numinous a part of our daily life, how to live with our own divinity.

Projection is responsible for much pain and misunderstanding in love affairs and marriages. We fall in love and marry our own projection, only to discover that we are living with someone whom we do not know and possibly do not even like. This can cause confusion and suffering, particularly if there is no understanding of the psychological drama that is being enacted. In many Eastern countries marriages are arranged and the animus/anima projection is not so influential. Although romantic love has existed throughout history and can be found in the literatures of different cultures, it is only in our Western culture that it is so dominant.[8] The idea of romantic love emerged in our Western culture at the end of the eleventh century in the poetry of the troubadours and the rituals of courtly love. Since then it has increasingly taken hold of our collective psyche, and today it fills the cinema and television screens of our mass culture. We believe in romantic love, enjoy its bliss, and are caught in its tragedy.

Is the answer to educate ourselves to withdraw this projection and never to marry when we are in love? Should we try to escape this gift, or is there a secret key that can unlock the conflict it creates (the dynamic of projecting an inner ideal onto an ordinary human being) and open up a higher possibility of loving? I once asked this question to a very wise old man, who replied with two words, "unconditional love."

For those who are prepared to suffer the depths of love, unconditional love can open a doorway that can lead us out of the inevitable disillusionment of projection. Unconditional love is all-inclusive. It does not demand but accepts. It is the quality of love described by St. Paul:

> Love suffers long and is kind; love does not envy, love does not vaunt itself, is not puffed up ... does not seek her own way, is not easily provoked, does not think evil of another ... bears all things, believes all things, hopes all things, endures all things.[9]

Unconditional love does not belong to the ego, for it transcends duality. Containing the opposites, the human and the divine, the person and the projection, unconditional love is not a peaceful state, for the lover is thrown between these opposites, confused and tormented by their contradictions.

What happens during this painful process is that in the alchemical vessel of the heart the lover's projections are burnt away together with the ego of the lover. The animus/anima returns to its place within the heart, not rejected but transformed through the fire. Then the lover sees in the eyes of his partner not the mystery of his own projection, but the beauty of her soul. The beloved can be seen as she really is, both human and divine. But now the inner attention of the lover is withdrawn and looks upon the Face of Another. The process that began through projection continues within the heart, and we begin to glimpse the real nature of our love affair; for the love for another human being is just a reflection of the only true love affair, the love affair with God.

The anima or animus appears from the depths of our unconscious and beckons us into the rites of love. For a man his own unknown soul puts on a human form, so that in the body of a woman he can adore and come to know his own inner feminine self. For a woman the masculine spirit of God touches her and in the form of a man takes her in its arms. In this alchemy we are confronted by the ultimate human paradox: that we are both human and divine. This is our greatest glory and our greatest suffering. Through falling in love we are able to touch the hem of our own divinity, enter into its timeless world in which a kiss can last forever. But each time we taste this wine, we also taste the pain of separation and the anguish that both we and our lover are human. We long to unite, to merge into the oneness of love, and yet we enact this mystery with another—with a human being who has feelings and desires that are often different from our own. Duality always remains, and on the human stage the ecstasy of love will always bring anguish.

The greatest love poems, *Romeo and Juliet, Tristam and Iseult, Layla and Majnun*, tell the same story: how love in this world is the tragedy of separation. Only in death do lovers unite forever. Death takes us beyond the ego and the world of opposites. Only then is there no separation. But the Sufi seeks to "die before death," because he knows that there is a Beloved who is not separate from him, but "closer to him than the vein of his neck."[10] If he can become free of the ego then he can become free of the chains of duality.

The path of love can take the wayfarer beyond the world of the ego. It is a painful process of burning until nothing remains. This is the state of *fanâ*, of annihilation. *Fanâ* involves the complete negation of the ego, the individual self, thus allowing a complete affirmation of the real and universal Self, as expressed by the Sufi formula, abiding after passing away *(al-baqâ ba'd al-fanâ)*. And this great journey often begins with the enigma of human love. A man once came to the Sufi master Jâmî and asked to become his disciple. He had studied all the scriptures in depth, and was very surprised when the master asked him, "Have you ever been in love?" He answered, "No." And the master said, "Go and fall in love and suffer, and then come back." The man went into the world and learned to love and suffer. Years later he returned to the teacher and eventually became his successor. To fall in love with the Infinite Nothingness is not easy. The Beloved takes us to Him from where we are standing and He knows that it is often much easier to first fall in love with a man or woman. In a human love affair our heart is opened, and then we are able to follow the path of love beyond the human lover into His burning arms. The Sufi says that all human love is learning to love the One Beloved. Just as girls play with dolls because one day they will be mothers, so do we fall in love and learn how to love each other, so that one day we will be able to love Him. In the words of Jâmî:

> You may try a hundred things, but love alone will release you from yourself. So never flee from love—not even from love in an earthly guise—for it is a preparation for the supreme Truth.[11]

He is a jealous lover and if He wants you for Himself, He will not let you be limited by a human lover. He will afflict you until nothing separates you from His embrace, as is implied by His words in the Qur'an, "And I have chosen thee for Myself."[12]

Yusuf and Zulaikha

If you really love someone, only that person exists and you yourself do not matter. This is what happened to Zulaikha when she fell in love with Yusuf. Yusuf is best known in the West as Joseph, the son of Jacob, who was sold into slavery in Egypt. There he interpreted Pharaoh's two dreams about the seven years of plenty and the seven years of famine and was made grand vizier. *Yusuf and Zulaikha* is one of the great love stories of the Middle East. It is described in the Qur'an as "the most beautiful of stories," and in the fifteenth century Jâmî turned this story into a poetic masterpiece which is a Sufi parable about love.

Jâmî begins his story about these two beautiful lovers by explaining how all earthly beauty is a reflection of the Absolute Beauty. When we fall in love we are caught by the rays of this Sun, and through the suffering of love we become open to its joy; through being the captives of love we become free. He then tells his love story through the eyes of the princess Zulaikha, who becomes love's captive through a dream. In her dream she sees with the eyes of her heart the vision of a most beautiful man. The Divine Lover takes the form of a man and plants love in her heart. She falls in love with this image and, captivated by its incomparable form, she is "oblivious to the underlying reality." But Jâmî tells his reader that reality peeps from behind appearances. We fall in love with the world of forms because in our hearts we know that it contains the Formless:

> When a thirsty man reaches for a jug, it is because he knows for certain that it contains liquid; but when he drowns in the limpid waves of the ocean, he no longer thinks of that weeping unglazed jar.[13]

Zulaikha falls in love with her dream and it drives her to despair:

> Pure jewel! You have carried off my heart, without telling me either your name or where you come from.... I have neither my own heart nor my heart's desire.[14]

In love we lose our heart to another and we lose our mind to love. The alchemy of love belongs neither to the world of forms nor to the rationale of the mind. (As e.e. cummings wrote, "love is a deeper season/than reason."[15]) Love is the deepest mystery in the world and can never be understood, for it is beyond understanding. Only one who is lost in love knows love, and if one is lost, there is no one to know anything. Zulaikha loses herself completely to a dream.

The Sorrow of Separation

Love that "brings wisdom to fools and folly to the wise" brings Zulaikha grief and sorrow. Without knowing its true meaning, she tastes the sorrow of separation. When we fall in love we are touched by our essence, which is love. We long to be united, and although we project this longing onto another, it is in reality a longing for our own inner partner, union with whom will bring wholeness. In a human love affair we can taste not only the bliss hidden in the heart, but also the pain of our own separation from the Source. This is why a love affair can be so painful, for we feel the deepest, most potent pain of our own incarnation. There is nothing more painful than separation, just as there is no bliss greater than merging into oneness. Separation is like a thread woven into the texture of our life. Sometimes it appears as dissatisfaction, as discontent with our ordinary life. But in the openness of love, it shows its true strength and can cause us unbelievable suffering. Only lovers who have paid with the blood of their hearts know this. Those who follow the path of love know this bleeding, but they also know that the pain of separation is the most direct route home.

From the moment Zulaikha first dreams about the divine aspect of her animus, separation fills her days. Then she has another dream in which her heart's desire appears and tells her he is the Grand Vizier of Egypt. Zulaikha is a beautiful princess, courted by many princes and kings. When she awakes from her dream she asks if any have come from Egypt and then tells her father of her love for the Grand Vizier. Her father sends envoys to Egypt to arrange her marriage. But the Grand Vizier turns out not to be the man she has dreamed of, but someone else. Imagine her distress when, still burning with desire for the unknown man she has dreamed of, she is forced to marry the Grand Vizier. Wedded to a powerful and wealthy man, she burns even more with the pain of suffering.

Then Yusuf is sold into slavery. When Zulaikha sees him, she realizes that this is the man of her dreams.

She buys him and thinks that the bliss of union is soon to be hers. But at this point in the story another woman, Bazigha, is overcome by Yusuf's beauty. She asks him questions to try and find the source of his beauty, and in his reply Yusuf explains that one should seek the true light and not its reflection:

> Hidden behind the veil of mystery, his beauty was ever free of the slightest trace of imperfection. From the atoms of the world he created a multitude of mirrors, and into each of them he cast the image of his face; for to the perceptive eye, anything which appears beautiful is only a reflection of that countenance.
>
> Now that you have seen the reflection, make all haste for its source; for in that primordial light, the reflection is entirely eclipsed. Beware of lingering far from that primal source; or else when the reflection fades you will be left in darkness. The reflection is as ephemeral as a rose's blush: if you want permanence, turn towards the source; and if you want faithfulness, seek it there also. Why tear your soul apart over something that is here one moment and gone the next?[16]

Only one Beloved is truly faithful; only one Beloved hears every cry, feels every tear. With Him each embrace takes us deeper and each time we are touched, it is with such tenderness. With Him the nearness gets greater and greater and it goes on forever. Through its reflections love can lead us to Him. Hearing Yusuf's words, Bazigha sees this secret truth, "that falling in love… is a mere allegory of reality." She sees behind the "veil of her desire," and, after spending the rest of her life in a hermitage, dies "beholding the splendour of the beloved."[17]

Zulaikha, however, can not escape her passionate desire to possess Yusuf. And she can not take the path of the ascetic. Her path is total absorption in her beloved Yusuf. She loves him so much that everything is he:

> Zuleika let *every*thing be the name of
> Joseph, from celery seed
> to aloes-wood. She loved him so much,
> she concealed his name
> in many different phrases, the inner meanings
> known only to her. When she said, *The*
> *wax is softening*
> *near the fire,* she meant, My love is wanting
> me.
> Or if she said, *Look the moon is up,* or *The*
> *willow has new leaves,*
> or *The branches are trembling,* or *The*
> *coriander seeds*
> *have caught fire,* or *The roses are opening,*
> or *The king is in a good mood today,* or
> *Isn't that lucky,*
> or *The furniture needs dusting,* or
> *The water-carrier is here,* or *It's almost*
> *daylight,* or
> *These vegetables are perfect,* or *The bread*
> *needs more salt,*
> or *The clouds seem to be moving against*
> *the wind,*
> or *My head hurts,* or *My headache's better,*
> anything she praises, it's Joseph's touch
> she means,
> any complaint, it's his being away.

When she's hungry, it's for him. Thirsty,
his name is a sherbet.
Cold, he's a fur. This is what the Friend
can do
when one is in such love. Sensual people
use the holy names
often, but they don't work for them.
The miracle Jesus did by being the name of
God,
Zuleika felt in the name of *Joseph.*[18]

Such identification with the Beloved is a mystical state in which everything belongs to love. Worldly lovers have their secrets, their special tunes and their shared intimacies. But for the mystic there is nothing other than Him; in everything His Name is written. The book *Mister God, This Is Anna* tells the story of a girl brought up in the East End of London before the Second World War who saw life in this way. She was totally fascinated by life because everything she saw and experienced told her about Mister God. The way light casts a shadow, the way mirrors can create an infinite number of reflections, or the magic of numbers—everything helped her discover more about Mister God. Anna understood the mystery that "God is our centre and yet it is for us to acknowledge that he is the centre.... Even while he is at the centre of all things he waits outside us and knocks to come in."[19] The more we see God in everything, the more we let Him into ourself. Too perfect to live, Anna died before she was eight. Just before she died she said, "It is like turning inside out." She had seen behind the veil of creation and glimpsed its inner secret.

Zulaikha loves Yusuf, longs for him, wants him. But he is very pure, and despite all her pleadings resists her. Zulaikha can see nothing beyond her own desire. She has not yet surrendered herself; she is still prisoner of her ego. To try to weaken Yusuf's resolve she has him thrown into prison and beaten. While in prison Yusuf engrosses himself in inner contemplation and Zulaikha loses herself more completely in thinking about him. She has imprisoned Yusuf, but even more is she his prisoner. Her heart is so filled with him that nothing else matters to her. The outside world has no meaning; there is no place in her consciousness for anything other than Yusuf. Just as the Sufi aspires to lose himself in remembrance of God, so is Zulaikha "so absorbed in the remembrance of Yusuf that she lost herself entirely; and the slate of her mind was wiped clean of all notion of good and evil."[20]

While Yusuf is in prison he becomes known as an interpreter of dreams. He is called to interpret Pharaoh's dreams about the seven fat cows and the seven lean cows. His interpretations bring him freedom and honor, and eventually he becomes Grand Vizier. Zulaikha's husband dies after seeing his fortunes fail. Zulaikha has now lost everything, both her husband's prestige and her beloved. She spends the remains of her fortune as gifts to those who bring her news of Yusuf and then she lives in a ruined hovel. She is left with nothing but the pain of separation and the name of Yusuf which is always on her lips. At this point she represents the stage of total desolation to which every wayfarer is brought. Everything is taken away; only grief and longing remain. In this state the only solace is the sacred name of the Beloved which is constantly repeated. Before He can fill our hearts we must be less than the dust at His feet. We must become nothing, we must be nowhere. As a friend was told in a dream, "You must reach the point of total despair." For only then does the ego finally surrender and so give space to Him. Two cannot live in one heart; either the ego or the Beloved must go, and the ego will only go "chased in sorrow and drowned in tears." Zulaikha's love for Yusuf brings her to this state: inwardly and outwardly she is totally destitute.

In her desolation Zulaikha builds a reed hut by the roadside, living only for a glimpse of her beloved as he passes by in his cavalcade. Her sorrow has taken away her beauty and love has cost her her free will. The little children tease and mock her, but she cares nothing for herself anymore:

> Have I not suffered separation long enough? What is left for me to sacrifice but sacrifice itself? How much longer must I remain cut off from the beloved? I would rather be separated from my own self![21]

Breaking a Projection

All that is left for Zulaikha is Yusuf's beauty. She has worshiped the image of his beauty, like an idol, all her life. One day when Yusuf rides past she crouches like a beggar woman by the roadside, longing to see his face. When he passes she lets out a cry from the depths of her heart. But, in the noise of the cavalcade, no one even hears her. This is the moment when her last attachment to the world of forms is shattered. She breaks the image which she has carried in her heart and washes it away with "her own tears and heart's blood." This image of her beloved, which long ago appeared in a dream, has taken her into the path of love. But too long has she worshiped this image and thus kept herself from the truth that lies behind it. Love has taken on the image of a beautiful man, but in worshiping the man, she has built a wall between herself and love. This wall has to be broken.

Through the dynamic of projection, an unknown, unconscious part of ourselves takes on the form of another. The shadow, the animus or anima, wise old man or woman—such inner figures come to meet us through our projections. This has a positive purpose, for it allows us to connect with these inner figures and get to know them—to feel their power, their wisdom, and also their darkness. If they were not experienced through projection, they would remain forever hidden in the unconscious, their energy undifferentiated. Through projection they become individualized and their qualities become familiar to us. But there comes the time when it is no longer helpful to project these energies; instead we need to integrate them, to acknowledge them as a part of ourselves. We need to take responsibility for these aspects of our psyche and use their energy creatively, even the energy of the shadow. The process of psychological transformation is a process of integrating the energies of the unconscious, and if our inner figures remain always as projections, their energy can never be integrated. The inner transformation is blocked.

But to withdraw a projection is not easy, and the longer a projection remains, the harder withdrawing it becomes, for the projection itself then becomes engraved within the psyche. It becomes a stone figure standing in our way. Furthermore, not only is it difficult to withdraw our negative projections, to acknowledge our own darkness; it is also difficult to withdraw positive projections. The animus and anima, and especially the Higher Self, are numinous, awesome energies; they are gods and goddesses. It is often easier to allow another to live out our transpersonal nature than to accept this energy as our own divine self.

The shadow is the dark side of the ego, but the animus and anima are archetypal figures and their energies take us beyond the ego. They are messengers of another world. This is why they are so powerful in projection, for they have the power of love. To fall in love is a wonderful gift which makes us seem to connect in the deepest possible way with another human being. We are not alone but linked within the heart to another. All projections have this quality of seeming to connect us with others; even in projecting our shadow we form a link. But because the animus and anima are our inner partners, in their projection we experience the shared intimacies of love. Even when, as with Zulaikha, the outer relationship is not fulfilled, the projection still evokes this possibility. It touches upon our own inner aloneness and our deep fear of being lonely.

To withdraw projections is a lonely process, particularly when the projection has brought the tenderness of a lover's touch, the warmth of another's heart. But there comes the time when we need to turn our attention to the inner world and embrace our own inner dynamism. This road that takes us into the beyond is the loneliest path; "two cannot walk side by side," and so often we are left seemingly desolate and isolated. But only in our inner aloneness can we be embraced by the Beloved; only when we are totally naked before Him will He take us in His arms.

At the beginning the projection, the image of the beloved, is a helpful focus for the energies of love. But eventually for the lover to reach the goal of love every effort must be made to tear away this veil:

> The final end of love is to become bare. As long as love is in the beginning stage of its journey, the lover's nutriment is supplied by the form of the beloved. However, once love reaches its final goal, it leaves behind every form. Just before this, the form of the beloved appears in its perfection and falls as a hindrance between the lover and love. Thus the lover must spend all his effort to remove this veil.[22]

Zulaikha breaks the image she has held in her heart and is thus open to experience love itself. She turns her attention from the gift to the Giver, to the One who has opened her heart. When Yusuf next passes on the road, she does not call out to Yusuf but to God. Only then do her words reach Yusuf and he feels their reverence. He calls her to come to him, and when he hears the story of her desolation through love, his prayer brings back her beauty. They are married and in her lover's arms she experiences the ecstasy of union. Zulaikha has sacrificed her entire life to love, and "a lifetime of obstacles had been melted down in the crucible of earthly love." Her path of love has purified her so that "when the sun of Truth finally rose, not a single obstacle remained." Her union with Yusuf is symbolic of an inner marriage in which her true Beloved takes her in His arms. Purified through suffering, she loses herself in the sunbeam that is love itself.

In *Yusuf and Zulaikha*, Jâmî tells of the lover and the Beloved, how He comes to her and makes her suffer. Through suffering her heart is made empty, empty of everything that is not He. Only the power of love can make the seeker suffer in this way, only longing burns everything away. One friend had a vision in which she saw that all the tissues of her heart were torn away, with only one string remaining. This string was for her Beloved to play, so that every moment of her life would be His music. It is a painful process, but is there anything else worth doing? Jâmî's final words are:

> If you are man enough for this path you must take your heart in hand. That, so the specialists say, is the only work worthy of the name.[23]

Layla and Majnun

While Zulaikha finally tastes the bliss of union, only in death does Majnun lie by the side of his beloved Layla. The story of Layla and Majnun is the best-known love story of the Middle East. Majnun means mad, for he goes mad for the love of Layla and spends his life wandering in the desert, composing poems about the tears he sheds for his beloved. Yet her name, Layla, means the dark one, which in that culture suggests that she is not even beautiful (though it could also have a deeper meaning, pointing to the dark side of the feminine and the pain that drives him to despair).

Layla and Qays (the youth's name before madness renamed him Majnun) meet at school and are childhood sweethearts. Qays becomes entranced by her and continually praises her beauty wherever he goes.

He has lost his heart to love and becomes called a 'majnun,' a madman. Layla loves him, but her family, fearing that his madness might dishonor her good name, separates them and keeps her at home.

Layla is the beloved, Majnun the lover, and his story is that of the seeker consumed by longing. In Nizami's version, written at the end of the twelfth century, their relationship is rich in Sufi symbolism—as when Majnun, driven by the pain of separation, creeps to Layla's tent:

> All the radiance of this morning was Layla, yet a candle was burning in front of her, consuming itself with desire. She was the most beautiful garden and Majnun was a torch of longing.... Layla could bewitch with one glance from beneath her dark hair, Majnun was her slave and a dervish dancing before her. Layla held in her hand the glass of wine scented with musk. Majnun had not touched the wine, yet he was drunk with its sweet smell.[24]

Majnun is the lover, consuming himself in the fire of his own longing, and his beloved holds in her hand the wine of love whose very scent intoxicates him. Layla, the dark one, has bewitched him, suggesting that she carries the power of the dark side of the feminine, which can overwhelm a man with the hidden mysteries of his soul. In the Christian tradition this esoteric relationship of the lover and the beloved is hinted at in Mary Magdalene's love for Christ, especially in their meeting after his death, when she mistook him for the gardener. Mary Magdalene also carries the dark side of the feminine, its rejected, passionate qualities. A love affair with God is passionate and all-consuming. The path of the lover is like that of Dionysus, the god of ecstasy who was born of fire. It takes us into the depths of the unconscious, into the dynamic and intoxicating darkness where both madness and bliss lie.

Majnun becomes totally intoxicated with love for Layla. His is the drama of love that burns everything away; he is "consumed in the fire of love, drowned in the tears of unhappiness." Imprisoned, the slave of love becomes lost. His one desire makes him an outcast in this world. Only those who have tasted such a wine can understand the consuming passion it evokes.

> Oh who can cure my sickness? An outcast I have become. Family and home, where are they? No path leads back to them and none to my beloved. Broken are my name, my reputation, like glass smashed on a rock; broken is the drum which once spread the good news and my ears now only hear the drumbeat of separation.
>
> Huntress, beautiful one, whose victim I am—limping, a willing target for your arrows. I follow obediently my beloved, who owns my soul. If she says "Get drunk," that is what I shall do. If she orders me to be mad, that is what I shall be.[25]

For Layla he has lost his reason. He is her victim forever. This story sounds familiar: is Layla la Belle Dame sans Merci? Has Majnun been caught in the enchantment of the siren and become lost in the dark waters of the unconscious? Does the witch now own his soul? Is this madness of love the same as being overpowered by the forces of the unconscious?

The lover's journey takes him into the ecstatic world of the inner feminine. One glance of the beloved's eyes opens a doorway into the world of love that lies beyond reason. But how does the mystic know that he is not being deluded by the mistress of illusion herself? Is there in fact any difference between being absorbed back into the waters of the unconscious, drowned in the embrace of the Great Mother, and being lost in the oneness of love? In both states individual consciousness ceases to exist; there is a feeling of primal unity as the oneness of life is experienced.

But between these two there is the greatest difference, for the mystic lover's madness is contained within the vessel of the Self. He has lost the consciousness of the ego so that a higher consciousness can be born. For the one who is caught in the embrace of the Great Mother, all consciousness is devoured. But the mystical journey is not into the womb of the Great Mother, but into the oneness of the Beloved, and she whose glance intoxicates the mystic lover is not the same as the siren. Layla, like Mary Magdalene, embodies the dark side of the feminine; she also points beyond it, for she has in her eyes the light of the Divine Lover.

The Crucible of the Heart

The intoxicating energy of the inner world is the ecstasy of Dionysus. To the ego this energy is destructive but for the soul it is bliss. The energy of Dionysus dismembers, tears apart the old structures of consciousness; in order for this energy to be creative, for this fire to give birth, it must be contained within the crucible of the heart. If the lover gives himself to love, seeking nothing for himself, longing only for the Beloved, then these powerful energies of the unconscious will transform him. It is the attitude of the lover that is all-important.

In the preceding chapter I stressed that the attitude of consciousness counterbalances the negative, destructive effect of the unconscious. However, the spiritual path points beyond ego-consciousness and there comes the time when the seeker must leave behind any mental or psychological security. Then the seeker focuses not on his individual consciousness but on the divine consciousness of the Self.

In turning away from the ego toward the Self, the lover forges a crucible that can contain the most powerful energies of the unconscious. Meditation, aspiration, and prayer strengthen this crucible, and constant witnessing or self-awareness stops cracks from appearing. Then, when the crucible is strong enough, it can hold the fire that reduces the ego to ashes from which the phoenix is born. Only if there is a secure relationship with the Self can this process take place; otherwise the energies of the unconscious will destroy the ego and nothing new will be born.

The Self is the master of the energies of the unconscious. Although the Self permeates the whole body, as a center of consciousness it is found within the heart. If we keep our inner attention focused on the heart, through meditation and aspiration we create a link with the Self; we allow It into our lives. Then the Self will use the energies of the unconscious to destroy the ego and all its attachments. If we surrender to this process and trust in the Self, we will be changed forever. The following story about a teacher and his disciple can be read as an allegory of this process. In the Sufi tradition the outer teacher always points to the inner teacher, the Self; thus this story tells how through love and devotion the disciple was killed and then reborn:

> The boy was the son of a disciple and the whole family were disciples of [the Guru]: father, mother, uncles, all of them. They were all sitting there, and also the Master, the Teacher of the boy. The boy had a natural smiling face; he seemed always to smile.... The Master looked at the boy and said: "Why are you smiling?" And the boy kept smiling. At that time everybody used to have a stick.... So, with the stick in his hand he began to beat the boy till the stick was broken. The boy kept the smile on his face. When the stick broke, he grabbed the heavy piece of wood with which wrestlers practice, and he continued to beat and beat till the head entered the shoulders and the shoulders into the body. One could not recognize who it was—nothing was there, just a mass of broken bones ... flesh and blood were everywhere. Then he stopped and said to the relatives of the boy: "What is this? Am I not at liberty to do as I like?"
>
> "Yes," they said, "we belong to you for life or death; you can do with us what you like." "Yes," he said, "I can do what I like," and he went inside. Some say he was sitting and chewing betel nut. Then he came out. "What is this?" he asked. "Who is lying here?" And, pointing to the mass of broken flesh which once was a human being, he said in a commanding voice: "Get up!"

> And the boy got up and was whole, and not a scar was seen on him. And he was told by his Teacher that from now on he is a Wali [Saint]. He was a Wali all his life.[26]

This was an actual incident, and the Sufi Master, Bhai Sahib, who witnessed it when he was a young man, explains its significance:

> You see, to make a Wali, it takes thirty or forty years. The physical body, the heart, the mind, is subjected to great suffering to clear out all the evils which are in the human being. And here the work was done in half an hour. How many evils were cleared away completely through such a terrible suffering. The boy loved him so much, always was sitting and looking at him. Never spoke before him. And was killed. Of course he was ready to be a Wali. Things are done in different ways according to the time and the people of the time.[27]

For most wayfarers the painful process of purification is experienced inwardly. The longing of the heart both burns us and keeps the attention focused on the beyond, on the Beloved who is our own Higher Self. Longing begins with an inward striving after selflessness, a deep desire to transcend the ego. According to Abû Sa'îd ibn Abî-l Khayr there is no way quicker to God than this. He describes it as

> a living and luminous fire placed by God in the breasts of His servants that their "self" *(nafs* or ego) may be burned; and when it has been burned [this] fire becomes the fire of "longing"

> *(shawq)* which never dies, neither in this world nor in the next.[28]

In the story of Layla and Majnun, Majnun's separation from his beloved fans the fire in his heart. That she is unattainable only increases his longing. When the Beloved appears in the form of a man or woman, love seems tangible, attainable. But this is only an illusion, and even in the moments of physical embrace, love can draw its veil, can hide itself. If love wants us for itself it will always beckon us into the beyond. The Great Beloved knows how to take us to Him. He knows the substance of our heart and can mold it as He wills. He knows that once we have had just one sip of the wine of love, we are lost forever; for us then the pain of longing is the sweetest sorrow. It is better than anything this world can offer. Majnun's father, driven to despair by his son's madness and sorrow, takes him on a pilgrimage to Mecca so that he may pray to be freed from love. But Majnun only asks that his love might grow stronger:

> They tell me: "Crush the desire for Layla in your heart." But I implore thee, oh my God, let it grow even stronger. Take what is left of my life and add it to Layla's. Let me never demand from her so much as a single hair, even if my pain reduces me to the width of one. Let her punish and castigate me: Her wine alone shall fill my cup, and my name shall never appear without her seal. My life shall be sacrificed for her beauty, my blood shall be spilled freely for her, and though I burn for her painfully, like a candle, none of my days shall ever be free of this pain. Let me love, oh my God, love for love's

> sake, and make my love a hundred times as great as it was and is![29]

Love has taken hold of Majnun and he lives alone in the wilderness. His longing transforms him; the fire of love burns away the ego. He is lost to this world, for love has turned his attention elsewhere. The ego gives us an identity, but before we reach the deeper identity of the Self, the identity of the ego has to go. When the ego has lost its grip the lover knows no longer who he is. Majnun's father comes to find him and bring him back to his family, but Majnun can only answer with the words of the mystic who is experiencing the states of confusion in which the only certainty is death:

> I have not only lost you; I no longer know myself. Who am I? I keep turning upon myself, asking, "What is your name? Are you in love? With whom? Or are you loved? By whom...." A flame burns in my heart, a flame beyond measure, which has turned my being to ashes. Do I still know where I live? Do I still taste what I eat? I am lost in my own wilderness.... I am drawn towards death—death is within me. If only you could forget that you ever had a son! If you could erase me from the book of those born into the world. If only you could bury me here and think: Some fool, some drunken madman.... What was to be expected of him?[30]

For the intellect such states are madness but to find a greater meaning we must travel beyond the intellect. On this journey everything is lost; everything is taken away and only paradoxes can point out the path:

In order to arrive at what you do not know
You must go by the way which is the way
of ignorance.
In order to possess what you do not
possess
You must go by the way of dispossession.
In order to arrive at what you are not
You must go through the way in which
you are not.
And what you do not know is the only
thing you know
And what you own is what you do not own
And where you are is where you are not.[31]

Majnun, consumed by love, ceases to exist. He becomes so absorbed by the object of his love that the lover and the beloved become one. In such a state there is no longer any separation: "If you knew what it means to be a lover, you would realize that one only has to scratch him and out falls the beloved." Rich with his love, Majnun cares for nothing else. In the wilderness he lives on roots, grass, and fruit, and having died to himself, is afraid of nothing. The wild beasts sense his unusual power, and, rather than attack him, befriend him. They forget their hunger and become tame and friendly. The fox, the wild ass, the lion, the wolf, and the panther travel with him and are his companions, watching over him when he sleeps. Majnun's love transforms the wildest animals, suggesting that within the lover the deepest, wildest instinctual forces are transformed through the power of love. These instinctual energies are not tamed by force, but as the fire of love alters the very structure of the psyche, they are integrated, contained within the all-embracing space of the heart. The heart is the king, and when the ego has surrendered, there are no battles or conflicts, because everything belongs and is accepted.

Majnun cares for nothing but love. He speaks his love poems to the wind, but others hear them and he attains fame as a poet. A young, romantic poet comes to visit him. However, he does not understand the depths of longing in Majnun's heart, and mistakes it for the youthful passion of romance. Romantic feelings can point us towards love, but they are like the moth which, seeing a lamp from afar, tries to describe the quality of fire. Only the moth that has flown into the fire and been burnt to ashes knows its real nature. The anima or animus appears and tempts us into love but every image must be burnt away; all duality must disappear. Then the Beloved merges into the heart of the lover. Majnun, speaking to this romantic youth, describes the painful path that has emptied him of everything, even himself:

> Who do you think I am? A drunkard? A love-sick fool, a slave of my senses, made senseless by desire? Understand: I have risen above all that, I am the King of Love in majesty. My soul is purified from the darkness of lust, my longing purged of low desire, my mind free from shame. I have broken the teeming bazaar of the senses in my body. Love is the essence of my being. Love is fire and I am wood burnt by the flame. Love has moved in and adorned the house, my self tied up its bundle and left. You imagine that you see me, but I no longer exist: what remains is the beloved.[32]

Layla dies before Majnun. He finds her tomb and dies there, his wild animals standing guard over his body. They have never been united in life, but through loving Layla Majnun has found a deeper unity than this world can ever bring. His love brings him to the same mystical state described by the Sufi mystic al-Hallâj, who was martyred for proclaiming "*anâ 'l-haqq*" ("I am the Truth"):

> I am He whom I love, and He whom I love is I.
> We are two spirits dwelling in one body,
> If thou seest me, thou seest Him;
> And if thou seest Him, thou seest us both.[33]

THE ALCHEMICAL OPUS III: SYMBOLS OF THE SELF

Somewhere there was once a Flower, a Stone, a Crystal, a Queen, a King, a Palace, a Lover and his Beloved, and this was long ago, on an Island somewhere in the ocean five thousand years ago.... Such is Love, the Mystic Flower of the Soul. This is the Center, the Self.

C. G. Jung[1]

SYMBOLS AND TRANSFORMATION

The energy of love reveals what was always hidden within the heart, the eternal secret of union. This is our essential nature, the Self, which the alchemists called the philosopher's stone, the *lapis*. The psychological and spiritual work of inner transformation is a process of uncovering this divine consciousness which exists within the heart, "that Person in the heart, no bigger than a thumb ... maker of past and future, the same today and tomorrow, that is Self."[2]

The Self is our innermost center, the part of our being that is not separate from God. This immortal substance exists within the "heart of hearts," the organ of divine perception that is within the heart *chakra*. The Sufi says that it is not the ego that makes the spiritual journey, but this mysterious substance which is both the pilgrim and the path. The Self awakens us to the call and then guides us on our way, leading us from the duality of ego-consciousness to its higher consciousness of unity. In the consciousness of the Self the knowledge and the knower are one, the lover and the Beloved are united.

The Self awakens us to our real nature and then takes us homeward. Without the Self there would be no awakening, no pilgrim, and no journey. The alchemists describe the paradoxical nature of this journey with the saying, "One must start with a bit of the philosopher's stone if one is to find it," and the Sufi expresses this same mystery with the saying, "The end is present at the beginning."

This awakening happens in the very core of our being as the Self turns our attention away from the ego back to Itself. Yet this happening takes place so deep within us that we have little direct consciousness of our own awakening, or of our higher nature that guides us. Also the Self is so powerful—it is like our Father in Heaven to whom we can pray—that until we have been prepared by the path we would be overwhelmed by even a glimpse of Its light. Instead the Self appears to us in dreams or visions as a symbol. The Self comes in many forms, in many different images, each image reflecting an aspect of our divine nature.

Jung's research into dreams and spiritual imagery documented many of the symbols of the Self. To name a few: an ordinary stone or the magical *lapis*; a crystal, whose mathematically precise arrangement suggests the union of extreme opposites—of matter and spirit;[3] the symbol of a mandala, suggesting the ordering principle of the Self; a helpful animal, representing Its instinctive nature and our primal connectedness to our surroundings;[4] or an elephant, whose great strength images the natural power of the Self. The celestial city is another symbol for the Self, as are the figures of Christ, Buddha, or other spiritual teachers; a wise old man or woman can also represent the wisdom of the Self.

In dreams the Self comes to meet us, not as an overwhelming power but as a symbol to which we can relate. But these symbols are not just images of the Self; they carry and communicate the numinosity and spiritual direction of our higher nature. They connect us to this deepest source of wisdom and power that exists within us. Symbols of the Self bring into consciousness what is hidden in our center and help in the work of transforming us, as the following dream and interpretation suggest:

> I dream that I am taken to a large room where there are a number of people, male and female. At one end sits a spiritual Teacher, who instructs us to go to the opposite side of the room where there is a large table covered with objects. All these objects are to be worn on the physical body, and will cause considerable discomfort, even pain. I remember seeing a hair shirt, and something to be worn around the head and fastened tightly. I choose a round pebble, to be placed in the shoe and worn all the time. I take the pebble and place it in my shoe, and walk towards the door. As I am leaving the teacher shouts after me, "It is possible to wear it, without it hurting too much."
>
> I awake from this dream feeling very "high," full of lightness and ecstasy. To ground myself somewhat I go for a walk, and all the time the symbology of the pebble haunts me like this:

> The pebble is a part of the stone, the symbol of the Self.
>
> It will make an imprint on my foot—a merging with the Beloved.
>
> The foot is a replica of the whole body, which will become impregnated with the Self.
>
> Ultimately there will be a complete merging between the pebble and myself—a oneness—the circle of the pebble will enclose my heart.

This dream points to the transformative power of the Self, and how in the form of a symbol it works within the psyche and everyday life of the dreamer—the pebble is to be "placed in the shoe and worn all the time." From a psychological perspective, how much the ego of the individual ultimately determines the actual dynamic of the individuation process is unclear. The ego can cooperate, responding to the energy of the Self and Its guidance offered in the form of intuitions, dreams, and hints. Then the conscious and unconscious work together in harmony. In fact, if the individual does not respond to the hints offered by the unconscious, the Self has the ability to attract external situations that force the individual to listen, even causing an illness or an accident. Jung said that if one does not deal with an internal situation, it can happen to one as fate. One just "happens" not to notice a red light...

Individuation is a powerful process, channeling energies from the depths of the unconscious. It is particularly important that the individual surrender to this process, and not hinder it with unnecessary resistance. This is reflected in the value the Sufi attaches to surrender, for it is the surrender of the ego to the higher

Self that both focuses the individual on the Self and allows the *opus* to proceed with minimum interference from the ego. Furthermore, it is the role of the teacher to point the disciple continually in this direction, to remind him of what is really important, as the following dream images:

> A woman has twins which die and this upsets me very much, and yet when I tell this to the teacher, she isn't very concerned. When I go to her flat I return some food which I had taken from there, but again this doesn't interest her very much. Instead she takes a dark stone from her pocket which glows bright and pulses with light and she says I should take this stone out from time to time and look at it.

In this dream, the dark stone "which glows bright and pulses with light" is undoubtedly the philosopher's stone, to which the dreamer has access, as the teacher tells her to "take this stone out from time to time and look at it." The philosopher's stone is always in our possession; it is only that it has been forgotten and needs to be uncovered. This dream also makes a valuable distinction between spiritual and solely psychological work. The "twins which die" and the "food which I had taken from her flat" suggest psychological disturbances within the dreamer, and yet the teacher is not interested, but rather turns the attention of the dreamer towards the stone. For the true purpose of the seeker is not to resolve all the problems of the psyche, but first to realize the Self and then to realize God. Realizing our divine nature we come into the presence of Him in whose image we are made.

Love is the central focus on the Sufi path, the unconditional love which belongs to the heart, the home of the Self. In the following dream the wayfarer's attention is dramatically turned away from her psychological problems, her neediness and anger, towards the real nature of the journey. She had this dream soon after she arrived at our Sufi group, and it showed her the essential nature of the path:

> Sitting with the group, I notice that bowls of food are being passed around, and one bowl contains a fresh salad that I feel very needy for. I am sitting next to my oldest friend, and as the salad comes my way she takes the last portion.
>
> As I am handed the empty bowl I go into a fury, and rush around the room sweeping things off shelves onto the floor, breaking them. I am consumed by rage and don't care about the consequences. Everyone is looking at me in disbelief that I can do such a thing, and then I begin to weep so deeply that it seems to come from the depths of my being.
>
> I look around the room and see what I have done. The room is in a mess with broken objects lying scattered over the floor. At this moment the teacher comes in. I am filled with shame, and say, "I am so sorry, so very sorry."
>
> The teacher looks around, and then flings open all the cupboards, and throws the contents all over the floor with the rest of the mess. She comes to me, puts her hands on my shoulders, and looking me full in the eyes, says, "It doesn't matter. Nothing matters except that we have love for each other."

We come to the teacher and the path burdened with our problems, our unmet needs and darkness. All our disturbances, neuroses, and shadow dynamics will come to the surface, to be accepted and loved. Yet the core of the path is not about psychological integration, but about the greater wholeness of love, a love that transcends boundaries and does not belong to the dualities of this world.

THE JOURNEY INTO DARKNESS

This love is always present, although buried, sometimes very deeply, under our conditioning and other psychological patterns. The substance of the Self is love, and it comes to us in many forms and images, turning our attention away from the outer world, back to the root of the root of our own being. This love is also the light of the Self, which will take us into the darkness, where our real nature is hidden. In the following dream of a woman in her early twenties, the Self comes to her in the image of a swan, which is a royal bird that mates for life. The swan beckons her away from the noisy party of outer life, towards a different horizon:

> I am at a party but I leave because I find it too noisy. I walk down to the beach, and there I see a swan swimming towards the setting sun. I become the swan.

Something within the dreamer draws her away from the noisy party towards the beach, where the waters of the unknown meet the dry land of consciousness. How often does spiritual life begin with a need for solitude, a need to withdraw into oneself? For only when one is alone with oneself can a new direction, a new depth of meaning, emerge from within. There, from the beach, she sees the swan, an image of her true, royal nature. A *hadith* (a saying attributed to the Prophet) states, "When you take one step towards Him He takes ten towards you." As the dreamer steps towards the path, the Self appears, which is both her guide and her goal. Becoming the swan, she begins her spiritual journey, leaving the shores of this world for the infinite ocean.

But why in this dream is the swan swimming towards the setting sun? Surely this departure should be towards the rising sun, symbolizing the dawn of a new consciousness. When I first heard the dream I was puzzled about this, but then I found the answer in an alchemical text quoted by Jung:

> "Know," says Ripley, "that your beginning should be made towards sunset, and that from there you should turn towards midnight, where the lights cease altogether to shine, and you should remain ninety nights in the dark fire of purgatory without light. Then turn your course towards the east, and you will pass through many different colours."[5]

And to this Jung comments: "The alchemical work starts with the descent into darkness (*nigredo*), i.e. the unconscious." Thus, symbolized as "a swan swimming towards the setting sun," the dreamer is embarking on the great journey into the depths of the unconscious, which is the work of a lifetime. Furthermore, this whole process begins with her identification with the swan: "I become the swan." She begins with recognizing her own higher nature, the *lapis*, and becoming one with it. Only the Self can take us Home. Instinctively, with a wisdom far deeper than the mind, we know that we need to give ourself to this process, allow oneness to lead us back to Oneness.

For those who are not on a spiritual path, their psychological *opus* will be consciously directed towards living in a more balanced and integrated manner, and indeed Jung stressed the importance of living "in *this* world, and *this* life."[6] Sufism is neither a monastic nor an ascetic path. The Sufi lives in the world, and may bring up a family, be a craftsman or businessman, yet his primary orientation is towards annihilation in God, a mystical state of union. And so, although the wayfarer's psychological work may reflect problems about living in this world, the *opus* is focused on the beyond. Thus, in the dream about the swan, the woman's journey (both spiritual and psychological) points away from the party of life and the shores of this world.

The Self is both the beginning and the end of the spiritual quest, a quest which takes the seeker far from the security of the known world. And yet the Self is something most natural, often imaged by a baby or divine child. The birth of the Self is a wonderful but painful process, for it is a stripping away of all of the illusions and identities with which we cover our real nature. In the words of love's martyr, al-Hallâj, "When Truth has taken hold of a heart she empties it of all but Herself."[7] The following dream alludes to this divine birth, and points to its "dark side." The central quality of this dream is a feeling of fear:

> There was a tremendous feeling of fear in this dream. Three old men got into my flat under false pretenses (saying that they were delivering a package) or they actually broke in. They were shabbily dressed and looked like hobos. They were small and they dropped off a package and then walked down the hallway looking in all the rooms. I was absolutely petrified and unable to speak. I tried to yell but nothing came out. I broke a glass, thinking I could use it as a weapon, and walked down the hall. They left and I rang the police so that they could be caught. I then opened the package that the old men had left behind, and while I was talking to the police, I saw that the package was in fact for me. There was a letter, but I didn't look at it. I was curious but still very frightened and suspicious to see what was inside. The first thing I saw was flowers. Then there were three gifts, beautifully wrapped in lovely paper. I opened one, but I think it had even lovelier wrapping paper inside. I was still frightened about the old men. The dream ended before I could see what the gifts were or who wrote the note.

The three old men leaving gifts echo three other men who brought gifts, gifts for a child born in a manger. The old men who looked like hobos are the Magi, and their gifts point towards the birth of the Self. In fact there is a suggestion that the Magi who came to honor the birth of Christ were early Sufis. They were the *Sophos,* the wise men from the East. There is a legend such men also came to Socrates, shortly before his death, to warn him of the danger he was in, and also visited Plato. It was said that these wise men used to move their lips in silent prayer, a custom which was not known to the Greeks. People would see them moving their lips without talking, and when asked, the *Sophos* said that they were praying. This is the silent *dhikr,* the remembrance of God, practiced by the Sufis.

But why were these three men in the dream dressed like hobos rather than kings, and why was the dreamer so frightened? Sufis are known as "travelers" or "wayfarers on the mystical path," following the saying of the Prophet, "Be in this world as if you are a traveler, a passerby, with your clothes and shoes full of dust." We are like tramps, not in the sense that we wear old clothes, but in the sense that we have no real home in this world because we belong somewhere else. We follow the will of God and not the ways of the world. This is simply expressed by the saying of Christ, "The foxes have holes, and the birds of the air have nests; but the Son of man hath not where to lay his head."[8]

It is not surprising that the dreamer is frightened by the old men. If one seriously embarks on the Path of Love, one becomes, like Majnun, lost to this world, wandering in the wilderness known only to those who have drunk love's wine. Maybe it does not happen so dramatically, but it happens. In fact the woman who dreamed about the hobos was already facing this crisis, in that she was in her mid-thirties, having given up a successful career in order to be with her teacher; and her mother was worried about her because she didn't have a proper job, or a house, or a husband, or children.

In the eyes of the world the Sufi is mad. We are in love with an invisible Beloved! We want the Nothingness!

We don't care about job, career, position, salary! All that matters is the greatest adventure, the path to the Infinite. And once you seriously begin, you can't go back. For there is nowhere to go back to. The world no longer exists as it used to. It no longer makes sense. And you have lost your old friends anyway, for they gave up on you. Your conversation and interests became boring. The other world that calls you is not even a distant dream to most people.

The three travelers, the hobos, give the dreamer flowers, gifts, and a letter. They bring a taste of the other world, a world without limits. They bring gifts of remembrance and awaken a fear that blinds the dreamer. This fear is very real, the fear of freedom, of leaving behind the known, the rational, the ways of the world. Once the heart is awakened, then the lover becomes homeless, for "the heart is ever restless until it finds its rest in Thee."

What do we do with this fear, this primal insecurity that often swamps consciousness with doubts? Do we have any defenses against our own sense of reason? How can we convince ourself that we are doing the right thing, when we don't even know what we are doing, where we are going or why? Every other journey has a sense of direction, but the lover only has longing, the sigh of the soul. We have to give ourself, recklessly, to our own longing, to this madness that has been born:

> Go forward, knowing the Path will vanish under you
> Open your arms, knowing they will burn away
> Give everything you are, knowing it is nothing
> Bathe always in His river, even when it's blood.[9]

Blinded by the Self

We give ourself to the craziness of love, to the path that is eternally present within the soul. We become a hobo, a wanderer, always in awe at what has been born within us. We are made blind to the values of this world, because we have glimpsed another. A simple dream describes this, and again there is the central image of a swan:

> A statue of a swan comes to life and starts to blind my eyes.

The swan, as symbol of the Self, begins to blind the dreamer to this world, because only then can the single inner eye, the eye of the heart, open to the world of Reality. The higher Self turns our attention away from this world, makes this world meaningless, before it can reveal a world that is not *maya.*

The dream starts with the swan as a statue coming to life. This reflects the fact that one begins spiritual life with the dim knowledge that one has a transcendent center of consciousness, but because one has little or no conscious experience of it, one creates a psychological image of the Self, a statue, which then awakens and has a life of its own. Creating an image of the Self is a necessary first step; indeed it is said that first you create an image of God and then God creates you; He then becomes alive within you and transforms you. Without this primary image of the Self, of our Lord, we would have no conscious sense of any inner direction, nowhere to turn. Of course the actual experience of this reality, the swan coming to life, will be totally different from any preconceived image, but the image forms an important conscious focus for the seeker; it will act as a nodal point in the psyche which helps to focus both consciousness and the unconscious towards the Self.

At the beginning the seeker forms some idea of what spiritual life is and to what he is aspiring. This idea may be formed from books or assimilated from various spiritual traditions, and it is a conscious direction which, combined with an inner discontent, longing, or aspiration, takes the seeker onto a spiritual path. However, once the seeker progresses on the path, such preconceptions will begin to go, for any true spiritual path will take one beyond the mind and its concepts. A conscious direction and idea about spiritual life is helpful at the beginning, forming a focus for aspiration, but it will dissolve as the real path comes to life within the seeker. Then, rather than any external or conceptualized image, the path becomes a living and dynamic reality within the psyche—the way and the pilgrim become one.

The Book of the Self

Although the path takes the wayfarer beyond any concept or image, there comes the time when some conscious understanding of the process is necessary. Like the lotus that gradually grows underwater, most of the work of transformation happens below or beyond the threshold of ordinary consciousness. But when the lotus reaches the surface, it flowers, opening to the sun; and similarly there comes the time when we need to know what is happening within us, when we need to take conscious responsibility for the light of our divine Self. The following dream describes how the dreamer is nourished by the unconscious but also needs to assimilate a conscious understanding of the path:

> I am invited to a meal. There are lots of beautifully cooked different foods, but there are also some books which I need to eat. I am slightly reticent about eating these books, but I eat some food, including a deliciously grilled fish. I then start to eat a book with a green cover and pictures of castles. I find that it tastes delicious. I embrace the woman friend who invited me to the meal and there is a feeling of great love.

The path offers much nourishment, of which the seeker is invited to partake; yet in addition to the cooked foods there are also books which she needs to eat. Books suggest conscious knowledge, and the dreamer would rather be nourished by the unconscious, "a deliciously grilled fish," than by these books. She is reticent about eating a book; there is an attraction in keeping the path hidden within oneself, unpolluted by the conflicts of consciousness and the arguments of the mind. This is particularly true for women, who have suffered only too much from the negative effects of masculine consciousness. When the mysteries remain hidden even from one's own mind, they will not suffer from the limitations of conscious understanding and the fragmentary effect this can have.

But the dreamer does "start to eat a book," one with "a green cover." Green is a very auspicious color, the color of growth and becoming; and, according to

Sufism, it is also the color of Khidr, the figure of direct realization of God. On the cover are also "pictures of castles" and castles, according to Jung, are symbols of the Self.[10] This implies that the dreamer needs to complement the unconscious nourishment offered by the path with some conscious understanding of what is meant by the Self. If we are going to follow the hints and inner guidance of the Self, of Khidr, in our conscious life, we need to have some understanding of what this may mean.

For many years after I came to the path I put away all spiritual books, and allowed the heart's secret love to change me without my knowledge or interference. But then one night I had a dream in which I was told to read the works of Jung. When I opened his books and read his description of the symbolic processes of individuation, I saw how some of these processes had happened within me, and I was filled with wonder. Many dreams rich in symbolism followed, and I came to have some understanding of my own transformation and the new consciousness that had been born. This understanding enabled me to live my outer life more in harmony with my inner nature. I began to glimpse the ways of the Self, and to take conscious responsibility for living this deepest essence.

Both my conscious and my unconscious joyfully responded to this new development. However, in many instances an inner drive towards consciousness may also be met with a certain resistance that can come from a reluctance to take responsibility for one's own spirituality. But when the dreamer actually eats the book with a green cover she finds that it "tastes delicious"; a conscious understanding of what is embodied in the Self must be one of the most delicious foods man can taste.

This book that the dreamer needs to eat does not imply that she needs to study texts, because everything in the dream is within her. The dream would rather suggest that she needs to make conscious what it means to live in relationship to the Self, to follow the way of Khidr. She needs to become conscious of her own innermost wisdom, the wisdom of the heart. Finally she embraces the woman friend who invited her to the meal. Whether this woman is an aspect of the higher Self, a helpful part of her personality, or an aspect of the shadow is unclear. (It is worth remembering that the shadow is not always unhelpful, and at times pushes us to become more conscious.) But what is important is that at the end of the dream there is "a feeling of great love," for the journey towards the Self is a lover's return to the arms of the Beloved, in whose embrace all the aspects of the psyche are contained in oneness and "great love."

The City of the Self

These dreams that contain symbols of the Self are infinitely precious because they form a bridge between ordinary consciousness and the greater wholeness of the Self that is hidden in the unconscious. Experiencing these symbols the dreamer connects with an inner reality that is, at that moment, still unborn, still separate from consciousness. From a Jungian perspective, an image of the Self acts as the "transcendent function," which is Jung's term for a function that facilitates a transition from one psychological attitude or condition to another. It bridges "the gulf between *consciousness* and the *unconscious*,"[11] enabling the Self and its accompanying psychological/spiritual condition to arise out of the unconscious and become manifest.

These symbols and images contain the seeds of this transcendent reality, seeds that can slowly germinate within the human being. They are infused with the dynamic energy of the Self, an energy that carries the stamp of our divine nature. Sometimes a dream will communicate not just an image of the Self, but an actual transcendent experience, as in the following dream. The dreamer is a man.

> I am with a woman whom I do not know personally, and I make a journey in search of something. We return to the high street empty-handed, having found nothing.
>
> I go directly to my teacher's house and enter the room which leads to her garden. She is in the room, standing by the wall at my left and wearing black.
>
> I look into the garden. As I do so the space in which the room, the teacher, and I exist undergoes a transformation, becomes a kind of "skeletal" space, in the matrix of which another dimension is revealed.
>
> I see a city that appears to be made of light, or permeated with light. Completely integral, the city in the distance is like a great palace, unitary, unfragmented, whole. I see the city from end to end. The light of which it is composed is fascinating but difficult to describe. There are different levels or dimensions of light. "Dimensions" not in the sense of geometric relations inherent in our experience of physical space and perspective. Rather it is *light-within-*

> *light*, so to speak; something I cannot explain in terms of the logic of perceptions familiar to everyday waking consciousness.

This dream begins with the theme of the search: the dreamer, together with an unknown woman, who is suggestive of his inner feminine, is searching for something which they do not find. Just as a previous dreamer left a party for the beach, so this dreamer, empty-handed, leaves the high street and its worldly values and goes directly to the house of his teacher, for what the dreamer is looking for cannot be found in the marketplace.

Entering the room which leads to the teacher's garden, the dreamer sees the teacher on his left, wearing black. Black is no color; it represents renunciation, or spiritual poverty, a total turning away from the world, complete dependence upon God. Ultimately black symbolizes a state of *fanâ*, annihilation in God:

> It has been said that mystical poverty is the wearing of black raiment in the two universes. This saying expresses the fact that the mystic is so totally absorbed in God that he has no longer any existence of his own, neither inwardly nor outwardly in this world and beyond; he returns to his original essential poverty, and that is poverty in the true sense. It is in this sense, when the state of poverty has become total, that a mystic can say that he is God.[12]

In the dream it is significant that the teacher is on the dreamer's left, for this is a feminine path that works through the unconscious, and even the relationship with the teacher takes place primarily in the depths of the psyche. In the presence of the teacher, the dreamer then looks into the garden, upon which "the space in which the room, the teacher, and I exist undergoes a transformation." The garden is an image for the inner world of the soul, particularly for the Sufi who sees in the beauty and sweet fragrance of the garden the reflection of an Infinite Beauty:

> What is all beauty in the world? The image,
> Like quivering boughs reflected in a stream,
> Of that eternal Orchard which abides
> Unwithered in the hearts of Perfect Men.[13]

In turning his attention away from the outside world towards the inner reality of the heart, the dreamer is shown that the teacher and her room are essentially a "skeletal" space within which another dimension can be revealed. This is a profound statement about the nature of a Sufi teacher who, "totally absorbed in God," is nothing but a space within which the seeker can realize another reality. Essentially the teacher does not exist.

What the dreamer experiences within this "skeletal" space is a city made of light, which the dreamer sees in its entirety, "unitary, unfragmented, whole." This experience is a glimpse of the Self, of his own divine nature in which everything has its true place, everything is included. On the level of the Self there is no duality, no sense of separation, only oneness. This "city" seen in the distance echoes the heavenly city of Jerusalem shown to St. John the Divine by an angel:

> And he carried me away in the spirit to a great and high mountain, and he showed me that great city, the holy Jerusalem, descending out of heaven from God.
>
> Having the glory of God: and her light was like unto a stone most precious, even like a jasper stone, clear as crystal.
>
> ...
>
> And the building of the wall of it was of jasper; and the city was pure gold, like unto clear glass.
>
> And the foundations of the wall of the city were garnished with all manner of precious stones. The first foundation was jasper; the second sapphire; the third, a chalcedony; the fourth an emerald;
>
> The fifth, sardonyx; the sixth, sardius; the seventh, chrysolyte; the eighth, beryl; the ninth, topaz; the tenth, a chrysoprasus; the eleventh, a jacinth; the twelfth, an amethyst.
>
> And the twelve gates were twelve pearls; every several gate was of one pearl: and the street of the city was pure gold, as it were transparent glass.
>
> And I saw no temple therein: for the Lord God Almighty and the Lamb are the temple of it.
>
> And the city had no need of the sun, neither of the moon, to shine in it: for the glory of God did lighten it, and the Lamb is the light thereof.[14]

In both the dream and the vision of St. John, the city of the Self is visible in its entirety, for the dreamer "an unfragmented whole," for St. John a mandala image. Furthermore, each description tries to convey a transparency and luminosity: the dreamer's city is "permeated with light," the heavenly Jerusalem is "pure gold like unto clear glass" and "the glory of God did lighten it." Finally, in both images there is a sense of different "levels": in the dream there are "different levels or dimensions of light," and in St. John's vision the city has different levels of foundation, seven in all. These levels of light are an attempt to convey an experience of a reality very different from our four-dimensional world. The dreamer insists that these "dimensions are not in the sense of geometric relations inherent in our everyday experience of physical space and perspective," and St. John's city is "coming down from God out of heaven," and thus its geometric proportions belong to another reality.

This dream of a city made of light points to the transcendent reality that lies behind the symbols of the Self. This is a dimension totally different from that of everyday waking consciousness; it is a world of *light-within-light* that cannot be described or explained in terms of our normal perception. This is why it is said, "Of those who make the journey no news returns." There are no words to describe the world of Truth. Yet the similarity of this dreamer's city to that experienced two thousand years earlier by St. John suggests that this inner reality has certain definite qualities of wholeness and luminosity, though they can only be hinted at.

For the Sufi, this inner world of light, "the Throne," lies behind the veil of the sensible world, and is reached through the heart. Within the heart is the light of the Self which, when the heart opens, merges with its source, the Divine Light of God. To quote Najm al-dîn Kubrâ:

> When this veil [the veil of creatural being] is rent and a door to the Throne opens in the heart, like springs toward like. Light rises toward light and light comes down upon light, *"and it is light upon light"* (Qur'an 24:35).[15]

Spiritual life is the simple process of unlocking the door in the heart. When this door is open, then His Light fills your life, and everything you experience becomes permeated with Him. His Light, which is none other than the Light of your own Divine Self, is reflected in the polished mirror of the heart.

The images of the unconscious are like keys which can open the door between the world of the senses and the numinous inner world of the soul. The symbols of the Self bring into consciousness the qualities that belong to our transcendent center, its mandala-like order, its luminous nature, its wisdom and power, and a freedom from the conditioned values of the world. Working within us, these symbols guide and transform us, revealing the deeper dimension of our own psyche. Imprinting themselves into us, they prepare us for a world beyond the known parameters of the mind and ego, a reality that is eternal and infinite.

From the beginning of the journey the Self calls to us. Arising from the unconscious, its symbols point the wayfarer beyond the duality of ego and shadow, beyond the dance of animus and anima. They reconcile the opposites of our nature, the conflicts of duality, and give us a taste of our primal wholeness. Activating the psychological process of individuation, the energy of the Self prepares us for union, the *unio mystica* in which lover and Beloved meet and merge into oneness. To quote Jolande Jacobi,

> The individuation process can "prepare" a man for [an experience of God in the form of an encounter or *unio mystica*]. It can open him to the influence of a world beyond rational consciousness, and give him insight into it.... One might say that in the course of the individuation process a man arrives at the entrance to the house of God.[16]

The images of the Self finally fall away as we cross over the threshold of our innermost being. The path of the mystic takes the lover beyond the psyche, beyond any image, beyond any form. Called by love we step into the oneness that lies within the heart, a merging into the formless emptiness of love. On this stage of the journey we are guided by love, and by those whom love has made empty. The mystic who is absorbed in God is an empty space within which others can safely come to know His eternal emptiness and taste the truth of their own nonexistence.

THE RELATIONSHIP WITH THE TEACHER

The world is full of beautiful things until an old man with a beard came into my life and set my heart aflame with longing and made it pregnant with Love. How can I look at the loveliness around me, how can I see it, if it hides the Face of my Lover?

Persian Song[1]

Without a Face, Without a Name

Once, when I was attending a Jungian conference in Georgia, I showed two video interviews of my teacher. A six-year-old girl was watching with her mother. When the first video was shown she looked for a few moments at the old woman on the screen and then went into a state of deep meditation, from which she was only awakened at the end of the program. However, when the next interview was shown a couple of days later, the little girl was wide awake, and after the interview had finished she asked, "What does she do besides talk?" I responded, "She gets inside people's hearts."

Before Irina Tweedie met Bhai Sahib, her Sufi teacher, she visited a French woman, Lilian, who was one of his disciples. She stayed overnight with Lilian, who the next morning received a letter from Bhai Sahib (posted at least seven days before) in which he wrote, "You are with a Russian lady and she has me in the heart of hearts."

The "heart of hearts" is the home of the Self. It resides on the right side of the physical body.[2] The teacher is in the "heart of hearts" because the relationship with the teacher takes place on the level of the Self. A friend woke up one morning and found that her teacher was inside her heart, so intimate and so near. Yet when she went that afternoon to the group meeting and saw the teacher sitting, talking to people, she was totally confused. Was this the same person who was within her own heart? The teacher sitting among all the people seemed in many ways so distant, so unapproachable. She always found it so difficult to talk to the teacher, to express herself; and yet within her heart there was such nearness.

The real relationship with the teacher does not exist at the level of ego-consciousness but on the inner plane of the Self. This relationship can be very confusing because it belongs to a dimension totally different from that of our everyday waking consciousness. The level of the Self does not belong to duality or the world of separation, and yet for many years the consciousness of the wayfarer remains caught in duality and separation. We may glimpse the real inner relationship, a relationship that belongs to the oneness of the heart, but not have the container to understand it. We may try to understand this inner connection in terms of normal human relationships, but this will only make us more confused.

The relationship with the teacher has a quality of intimacy that reflects the inner experience of the oneness of the Self, a oneness in which individuality is not lost but retains its essence. The Beloved who is *one* and *alone* is manifest in the divine individuality of the Self. At this level we are totally alone and at the same time totally one with the Beloved, and also with the teacher who is His representative. This union at the level of the Self is closer than sexual union because there is no separation, and yet at the same time it is *totally* beyond the level of the personality. It is an *impersonal* relationship. On the level of ego-consciousness we relate through our personality, and therefore any closeness and intimacy has a personal dimension. The closeness of the inner relationship with the teacher is reflected into our waking consciousness; the wayfarer feels the "soul intimacy," and tries to relate this feeling to the normal patterns of ego-consciousness, tries to give it a personal dimension. But because this relationship does not belong to the ego there is no recognizable pattern into which it will fit, and the wayfarer is often left in a state of confusion.

The real relationship with the teacher is from heart to heart, from soul to soul. And the most fundamental part of this relationship is that the teacher is *not there.* The teacher is just an empty space through which the Beyond, the Infinite Emptiness, can be experienced. There can be no relationship with the teacher on the level of the personality, because the teacher is one who has been made empty, who has been made "featureless and formless." Because the teacher is empty, has passed away and is free from self, the teacher is a space in which the lover can meet the Beloved.

A teacher, or guide, is essential. If you need a guide to cross an unknown land, how much more do you need a guide to help you through the unknown inner world! To quote Rûmî: "Choose a master, for without him this journey is full of tribulations, fears, and dangers. With no escort, you would be lost on a road you would have already taken. Do not travel alone on the Path."[3] The teacher calls to the inner being of the seeker, awakening the hidden substance of the heart, saying, "Yes, you can make this journey. It is not an impossible dream, but a reality. I have been there and I know." The teacher's being speaks its own experience directly to the heart of the seeker, and the heart of the seeker responds. The heart of the seeker knows that its deepest longing is being spoken to, that its most precious desire can be realized. The teacher calls to the seeker not with the voice of the personality, but with the song of an ancient spiritual tradition, with the song of all those who have gone before. The Sufi teacher is the human representative of a lineage, of a spiritual line of masters, each merged into the other. Each Sufi is a ray of energy that links the wayfarer to the many great masters who have gone before us; and these great beings look after us, help us to walk the lonely and desolate path home.

As the human representative of a lineage, the teacher often appears as the physical focus of the wayfarer's attention. The teacher holds the aspiration of the seeker, knows the heart's deepest longing. The teacher encourages the wayfarer, increases the longing, and confuses the mind. A woman once said to my teacher, "I have this terrible longing, and I come to you because I hope it will grow less." My teacher said nothing; she smiled to herself, because she knew that each time the woman came the longing would increase. It is the job of the teacher to feed the fire of longing within the heart and to keep the wayfarer's attention always on the path.

The teacher is the focus of attention because he or she has been made empty. It is not the teacher who calls to the seeker, but the Emptiness which beckons. For the mind this is incomprehensible and very disturbing, because paradoxically the effectiveness of the teacher depends upon there being no one there. In the Sufi tradition the teacher is "without a face, without a name." It is the teaching and not the teacher that matters, and yet this is a teaching which is conveyed not through words but through the very essence of the teacher. The essence of the teacher speaks to the essence of the seeker, and it speaks the most intimate things: the mysteries of the heart, the intoxication of the soul.

I once had a dream in which I said that the only way I could possess my teacher was when she turned into a basket of bread and wine. If the teacher is to convey the essence of the path, there must be no attachment to personality—only an openness to the inner nourishment that is offered. Attachment to the personality of the teacher will only limit what can be given. If something is named, it is limited. This is why, according to the ancient tradition, the disciple never speaks the name of the teacher. One friend called Alex had a dream in which he was led to an Indian man who stood behind a bar. He was introduced, "Alex, this is Mr. So and So." The man behind the bar had no face. When Alex woke up, he was very puzzled; the man had no face and Alex didn't know his name. The bar or tavern symbolizes "the heart of the perfect Sufi, the master who has realized Union with God," and it is also the "house of the master."[4] The bartender is of course the master, the teacher who can give the dreamer spiritual intoxication:

> Be drunk, wasted away on the wine of
> God-yearning
> For this divine wine contains no hangover.[5]

NEITHER OF THE EAST NOR OF THE WEST

The teacher is a visible link with the Beyond, someone who carries the authority of a spiritual tradition and appears to personify the path. Yet when one friend first came to our group she was given a dream that alluded to the deeper mystery hidden within the presence of the teacher:

> I enter a room where people are sitting. There are two men; one has more authority. He has white hair and a white beard. He is either white or light. The other man is younger. He is neither of the East nor of the West. Between the two is an empty space and all the people sitting in the room are looking towards the empty space.

In this dream the actual physical teacher, an old woman, is not present. All the people in the room are looking towards an empty space. The dreamer's unconscious knew the esoteric truth that the teacher is just an empty space and was telling this to her conscious mind. It gave her an inner glimpse so that she would not get attached to the outer form of the teacher.

But at the same time the dream points to something deeper. The dream's description of the two men who sit on either side of the empty space directly alludes to a passage in the Qur'an, although the dreamer belongs to a Hindu family and had no conscious knowledge of the Qur'an. One man was "either white or light" and the other "neither of the East nor of the West." In the Qur'an (24:35) it is written:

> Allâh is the light of the heavens and the earth. His light may be compared to a niche that enshrines a lamp within a crystal of starlike brilliance. It is lit from a blessed olive tree that is neither of the East nor of the West. Its very oil would almost shine forth, though no fire touched it. Light upon light; Allâh guides to His Light whom He will.

Like all passages in the Qur'an this verse can be interpreted at different levels. But in relation to the dream it alludes to the mystery of the deepest relationship with the teacher, in which the light of God shines through the teacher and calls to His light within our heart. There is only one light, which is "the light of the heavens and the earth." Yet His light is hidden within the niche of our hearts, waiting to be called, waiting to be evoked. The teacher is one within whom His light shines brightly, for there is no veil of the ego to hide it. When the light within the teacher calls to the light within the seeker, the seeker's light burns more brightly: "Light rises towards light and light comes down upon light, 'and it is light upon light.'"[6]

We cannot see our own light except through His light. In the Psalms it is written "in thy light shall we see light."[7] It is through God's grace that He provides the light in which we can see our own light: "Allâh guides to His Light whom He will." The teacher, being one with God, is His representative and does this work for Him—if He wills. And the substance of this light is love. The teacher evokes love within our heart; he calls to our heart and the hidden longing within our heart responds. As our heart burns brighter with longing, so the fire in the Beloved's heart burns for the lover:

> Each time the heart sighs for the Throne, the Throne sighs for the heart, so that they come to meet.... Each time a *light rises up from you, a light comes down toward you,* and each time a flame rises from you a corresponding flame comes down toward you.[8]

The teacher gently blows on the spark that exists within the heart until this spark becomes a burning fire that consumes the seeker. Because in the beginning this fire is easily put out by the distractions of the world, it is the job of the teacher to keep it burning. But there comes the time when the fire has burnt away enough of the ego that there can be no resistance; nothing can put out its flames. Then the seeker is taken over by the process and there can be no going back. No longer is there any need to blow on the flames, for spiritual life has become an all-consuming passion. The seeker is then fully in the hands of God. This is the secret of the mystical approach *(sirr al-sayr),* when "the substance of light in Heaven yearns for you and is attracted by your light, and it descends towards you."[9] Finally the light within the seeker and His light merge and they become one light. The relationship with the teacher also ceases to be a duality. The seeker merges into the teacher and their hearts melt together. This is the end of the training, when the Higher Self of the seeker is united with the Self of the teacher.

Surrender to the Teacher

The wayfarer on the Sufi Path seeks to be in a state of continual absorption, merged within the teacher who is merged with the One. Through merging with the teacher *(fanâ fî'sh-shaykh)* the seeker then merges with the Prophet, not as man but as Essence *(fanâ fi'r-rasûl)*, and then finally merges with God *(fanâ fî Allâh)*. The whole process is the work of a lifetime, but the first stage, merging with the teacher, is the most difficult: "From the moment you are united with the Master, it becomes completely effortless."[10] Before union with the master great effort is required, because it involves the complete surrender to the will of the teacher, which is the first step leading to complete surrender to the will of God. "Surrender is the most difficult thing in the world while you are doing it, and the easiest when it is done."[11] The ego has to learn to bow itself before the Self. Once the ego has learned to surrender then He takes over, and "how can there be effort with Divine things?"[12] Through surrendering to the will of the teacher, who is one with God, the seeker overcomes the greatest obstacle for spiritual life:

> To be a Sufi is to give up all worries and there is no worse worry than yourself. When occupied with self you are separated from God. The way to God is but one step: the step out of yourself.[13]

One friend saw this surrender imaged in a dream he had soon after he met his teacher:

> I walk out of the house and meet the teacher on the street. She points a finger at me and says in a stern voice, "You are not in control anymore. I am."

Surrender is a very disturbing process because it involves the ego's giving up its precious autonomy. It is a death, and like physical death is accompanied by deep fear of an unknown beyond. But just as one who is not frightened of death can help another to die, so does the very presence of a teacher who is surrendered to God make it easier for the wayfarer to surrender. I was once clearly told, "It is easier to surrender in the presence of one who is surrendered." The being of the teacher radiates the inner security that can come only from this ultimate sacrifice. In this way the teacher invisibly supports the wayfarer during this period of transition.

In essence the surrender is not to the outer teacher, who, like any human being, will have faults, but to His light which is within the teacher. This light within the teacher is the same Divine light that exists hidden within the seeker. In surrendering to the light within the teacher, the seeker is therefore surrendering to the light of the Self that is within his own heart. Because at the beginning of the quest the wayfarer's own light is too veiled to be directly perceived, it is more easily experienced as a reflection in the clear mirror of the teacher's heart.

Because the purpose of surrendering to the teacher is to surrender to one's own inner light, it is very important to find a teacher who is free from self (whose ego is surrendered to God), who is "not there" and will therefore mirror the light of the wayfarer's Higher Self without getting in the way. The Indian saint, Anandamayi Ma, describes how precious it is to find such a guru:

> Finding a genuine guru is indeed a blessing. One must follow his advice unconditionally. While obeying the guru and treating him with reverence one must not become attached to his personality. The true guru will naturally emphasize the fact that he is merely the vehicle of God

> and discourage personal veneration. It is the false guru—still in ego-consciousness—who permits the development of a personality cult.[14]

The danger of a false guru is that the seeker surrenders his will to the will of another, rather than to an empty space in which the seeker's will can be embraced by God. It is in the empty space within the teacher that the transformation of the seeker's ego takes place.

The Process of Projection

An important part of the relationship with the teacher is often the process of projection. The dominant role of the teacher makes him a "hook" for many different types of projection, the most frequent of which is the projection of the Self. The Self is something so awesome, so luminous and dynamic, that at the beginning it is very difficult to own it as a part of ourselves. Rather than acknowledging that we have this inner wisdom and guidance, it is easier to project it onto the teacher, who is supposed to be full of wisdom and light. Through the projection a previously unknown, unacknowledged part of ourselves becomes conscious, even if it appears to belong to somebody else. Projecting the Self onto the teacher, the seeker is able to form a relationship with his divine light, as is often apparent in dreams in which the teacher images the Self. Thus, through the relationship with the teacher, the seeker will be able to connect and become familiar with the Self, without being overwhelmed by the true nature of his inner being.

However, there comes the time when such a projection is a limitation, when it is time for us to fully acknowledge our own divinity and learn to live in relationship to the Self without the mediation of the teacher. A year or more after the dream in which the teacher told him he was not in control anymore, the same man had the following dream:

> Sitting with a small group of people, the teacher asks, "What do you need from me so that you don't need me anymore?"

The teacher is like a ferryman who helps the seeker to cross over from the outer to the inner world. But once the seeker has arrived on the shores of his inner being, the ferryman's work is done. The wayfarer must then leave the boat behind, and, standing firmly on his own feet, journey on, for the road itself is infinite. In the words of Bahâ ad-dîn Naqshband:

> We are the means of reaching the goal. It is necessary that seekers should cut themselves away from us and think only of the goal.[15]

On the inward path any outer relationship is a limitation. The outer teacher only points to the inner teacher, the aspect of one's own being that is one with God.

In the Zen tradition it is said, "If you meet Buddha on the road, kill him." As the wayfarer travels "from the alone to the Alone," he reaches the stage when there should be no reliance on an outer teacher, and any such projection must be withdrawn. In our group many people have dreams of the teacher dying. This points to the death of the projection onto the teacher and the integration of whatever was projected. One friend, whose teacher had actually physically died a few years before, had a dream in which he saw his teacher,

Babaji, sitting in a chair, dead. Then he came alive again, and the dreamer said to him, "You must be a great yogi to come back from the dead." Babaji replied, "I am not a great yogi. I am you."

The teacher can only point us back to ourselves, away from the world of duality into the oneness of the Self. Yet when the teacher "dies" this does not mean the end of this relationship but rather its transformation. A relationship in which there was duality merges into oneness. The teacher and wayfarer merge together as the wayfarer experiences what was always, in fact, the true nature of this relationship. The call and the echo are one. The light within the teacher calls to the light within the seeker but it is really one light, calling to itself, evoking itself. Within the heart it is "light upon light."

A Closed Circle

The teacher is a mirror in which the seeker can first glimpse, then slowly become familiar with, and finally recognize, his Real Self. The teacher sees this inner potential from the very beginning, and whatever the outer appearance, relates directly to this essence. The relationship of the true teacher to the seeker is one of love from essence to essence. As such it can never change but is always complete:

> Love cannot be more or less for the Teacher. For him the very beginning and the end are the same; it is a closed circle. His love for the disciple does not go on increasing; for the disciple, of course, it is very different; he has to complete the whole circle.... As the disciple

> progresses, he feels the Master nearer and nearer, as the time goes on. But the Master is not nearer; he was always near, only the disciple did not know it.[16]

The teacher embraces the whole of the seeker, accepts him in his entirety, without judgment and without comparison. The teacher takes the seeker from where he is standing, and through the process of reflection guides him on the path back to himself. Seeing the full potential of the seeker, the teacher holds that potential regardless of whatever self-doubts the seeker may have. Even when the seeker seems to fail or deviate from the path, the teacher still believes in his spiritual capability—his capacity to be filled with God—and holds that belief as in trust until the seeker is able to realize it for himself. The teacher can never reject the seeker, just as God can never reject a human being, for we are all part of Him.

At times the teacher needs to be hard and cruel, even to appear to reject the seeker, but this is only to help the seeker to grow: "The Master must be strict, he has to be hard, because he wants the disciple to reach the highest state."[17] In particular, if the seeker is not able to withdraw the projection of the Self when it is necessary, if the seeker becomes too dependent on the teacher, the teacher may need to throw the seeker back upon himself. In the Sufi system the seeker may be thrown out of the group; according to the tradition this person should then be left alone by the other members of the group in order to realize his own inner strength. If the group as a whole is projecting too much upon the teacher, the teacher traditionally just disappears. One day people arrive for a meeting but there is no one there. Nobody knows where the teacher has gone or for how long. It can be for two weeks, two months, or even a year. Then, when the time is right and the group has learned to be more self-reliant, the teacher will reappear. Through outer insecurity the wayfarer is able to reach a greater degree of inner security.

The teacher must always be free from outer constraints so that at any instant he can follow the hint, even if this means leaving in the middle of a conference or appearing to abandon people at the time of their greatest need. But if at these moments the seeker fully surrenders, he will find that the inner connection with the teacher has grown stronger. In his outer absence the teacher is inwardly more present. Through being outwardly rejected the seeker realizes the real inner link which has always been there and belongs to neither time nor space.

The False Guru

Even when the teacher figure is not free from the ego, the projection of the seeker's Higher Self onto the teacher can still take place, but there is the danger that this projection can get caught and not be able to be withdrawn. The projection of the Self onto another invests that individual with a certain power, which could gratify the ego. If this happens, the teacher figure might not want this projection withdrawn and could subtly encourage the seeker to remain dependent. As in psychological analysis, the relationship with the teacher usually involves a "transference." The teacher carries the projection of the seeker, but unlike in analysis there should be no "countertransference" (i.e., there should be no projection by the teacher onto the seeker). The teacher should not be attached to the role of teacher, nor project the role of disciple onto the seeker. The seeker must be left free.

If the teacher figure is in any way attached to the role of teacher, he will not be able to reject an individual at the moment when it is necessary to break this projection. If there is any ego gratification from his position he will not be able to abandon the group at the right moment. In the inner dynamic of both, the individual and the group, moments arise that must be grasped in order for the full potential of a human being or a group to be realized. The true teacher is one who is both free and fully surrendered, so that when the hint is given, when the moment is right, he acts without hesitation or self-concern. Often the teacher will have to follow a hint which he does not understand at the time and which may even seem to be against his best interests or those of the seeker.

However, even though there are these dangers if one has a teacher who is not free from self, it is the attitude of the seeker that is all-important. For one who aspires and is humble enough to accept what life brings and to go beyond any feelings of resentment, a false guru can be a stepping stone to a true teacher. Indeed, a seeker can even realize God through a false guru:

> What if one has unwittingly found a false guru? Even this is only seemingly a misfortune for there will come a time when one awakens from one's error and then one will assuredly know how to discover a genuine guru. There is another aspect to be considered. More important than the guru is the devotee's own attitude,

> because in the ultimate sense no one can give us Self-realization. We have to find it. Thus it is that a sincere seeker, seeing God behind his guru, however imperfect that guru might be, will be able to go beyond the guru and reach God.[18]

Through the process of projection the seeker sees the teacher as an image of his own deepest aspirations. If the seeker has sufficient faith in this image and stays true to his aspirations, he can go beyond the form of the teacher to find his own divinity; he can see his own true face reflected back. There was once a poor Indian woman who needed to visit her sick son. But he lived on the other side of the river, which was in flood, and the ferryman would not take her across. On the rocky banks of the river a holy Brahmin was performing a fire ceremony with the ritual incantations. The poor woman approached him to ask for some divine charm to help her to cross the river. The Brahmin, not wishing to interrupt his sacred ceremony and thus have to repeat the complicated ritual, wanted to get rid of her as quickly as possible. "Just repeat 'Ram, Ram,' and you will cross the river," he told the old woman and returned to his incantations. Later, as the evening sun was setting, the Brahmin was still sitting beside the river, having finished the sacred ceremony. He was surprised to see the old woman again approaching him and was even more surprised by the look of joy and reverence on her face. She bowed before him and said, "Oh holy one, so great are your wondrous powers. Repeating 'Ram, Ram,' I walked across the river and was able to stay and comfort my son. Again repeating the sacred syllables I returned back across the river. I offer eternal thanks for your divine aid." The Brahmin looked at the old woman in astonishment and wonder.

So great had been her belief in him that it had carried her across the flooded waters. He felt humbled before her and the power of her faith.

THE CALL OF THE SELF

The teacher is a stepping stone, allowing the wayfarer to cross from the world of the ego into the larger dimension of the Self. Through the relationship with the teacher the Self is brought closer to our consciousness, and the ego is attuned to its faster vibrations. As the seeker's attention is slowly shifted from the ego to the Self, he learns to live constantly listening to the hints that flow from within.

The Self is the core of our being. As much as it is "smaller than small," hidden within the heart, so is it "larger than large," embracing and permeating every cell of the body, every aspect of the human being. It is continually sending messages to the ego, trying to guide it and point it towards the goal. However, if someone is not interested in spiritual life, sees the world of the senses as the only reality, his ego will cut him off from this continual stream of inner guidance. A friend had this explained to him by a voice in a dream:

> People with a strong sense of ego cannot lead a guided life. Their life is guided by the will of their ego and therefore it is impossible to allow anything else to come in.

If the ego does not acknowledge the existence of any consciousness higher than itself, then there is no relationship between the ego and the Self. The Self still continually tries to connect with the ego but the ego walls itself up. So the Self remains an onlooker, bored by the limited perspective of a human being who does not acknowledge the limitless world of his inner being, who remains a prisoner in a world of time, caught between the opposites of life and death.

The spiritual quest begins when an individual turns his attention away from the outer world of illusion and listens to the call of the Self:

> I am calling to you from afar;
> Calling to you since the very beginning of days.
> Calling to you across millennia,
> For aeons of time—
> Calling—calling.... Since always....
> It is part of your being, my voice,
> But it comes to you faintly and you only hear it
> sometimes;
> "I don't know," you may say.
> But somewhere you know.
> "I can't hear," you say, "what is it and where?"
> But somewhere you hear, and deep down you
> know.
> For I am that in you which has been always;
> I am that in you which will never end
> Even if you say, "Who is calling?"
> Even if you think, "Who is that?"
> Where will you run? Just tell me,
> Can you run away from yourself?
>
> For I am the Only One for you;
> There is no other,
> Your Promise, your Reward am I alone—
> Your Punishment, your longing
> And your Goal.[19]

Always the Self calls to us, whether we listen or not. This call is our friend; it is the thread that will lead us home. But, as in the words of this Persian song, it is also our punishment. The Self is the enemy of the ego, demanding its surrender. For this reason the ego will never instigate the journey that leads to its own death. We listen to the inner call only because He wills: "Allâh guides to His Light whom He wills." Someone said to Râbi'a:

> "I have committed many sins; if I turn in penitence towards God, will He turn in mercy towards me?"
>
> "Nay," she replied, "but if He shall turn towards thee, thou wilt turn towards Him."[20]

The Teacher Does Nothing

The teacher always points us away from the ego into the beyond, which is none other than our own simple essence. I mentioned earlier how a friend had two dreams which described the beginning of this journey. In the first dream the teacher said, "You are not in control anymore, I am," and in the second asked him, "What do you need from me so that you don't need me anymore?" This dreamer had a third dream which amplified the other two:

> The teacher takes my expired driver's license and throws it away. Then she says, "I can't do anything more for you." I ask, "What can I do for myself?" She replies, "Nothing."

The dreamer's driver's license imaged his life "driven" by the ego. So often we are the slaves of our own ego, driven by its desires. Spiritual life means learning to be free from the ego and its attachments. For the dreamer this ego identity had "expired" and was thrown away. He was free for a different "driver" to take over and direct his life. It seems from the dream that the teacher's work is now done; she has helped destroy the patterns of the ego and can do nothing more. The dreamer is also told that he can do nothing for himself either. Yet this dream does not mean that the dreamer has either reached the goal or been abandoned. Rather, it points beyond ego consciousness to the Self, which is not about doing, but is a state of being.

The teacher does nothing, for even the desire to help creates a barrier. My teacher calls herself "the caretaker of her apartment"; she just looks after a space in which the sincere seeker can come closer to his or her essence. In this space people change; it is "a house of drunkards and a house of change." For those who stay, mysterious and wonderful things happen in their innermost being and sometimes also in their outer life. People are healed, both physically and psychologically. Obstacles that impede inner growth are removed; life becomes richer and more complete. But the teacher herself does not do anything; rather "things are done." People do not believe her when she says that she is just a caretaker, for they like to project onto her all kinds of special abilities and powers. The reality of spiritual life is often too simple to be fully appreciated. Anandamayi Ma describes the function of the teacher in the simplest, most natural imagery:

> What this child would recommend for you is to sit under a tree. By tree I mean a real saint. A saint is like a tree. He does not call anyone, neither does he send anyone away. He gives shelter to whoever cares to come, be it a man, woman, child or an animal. If you sit under a tree it will protect you from the weather, from the scorching sun as well as from the pouring rain, and it will give you flowers and fruit. Whether a human being enjoys them or a bird tastes of them matters little to the tree; its produce is there for anyone who comes and takes it. And last but not least, it gives itself. How itself? The fruit contains the seeds for new trees of a similar kind. So, by sitting under a tree you will get shelter, shade, flowers, fruit, and in due course you will come to know your Self.[21]

The teacher just is and so allows the seeker to find that same innermost core within himself. One friend had a vision of the teacher as a tree. As more people came, the tree put out more branches. Some people were close to the trunk; others were out sitting on the ends of branches, talking among themselves. Still other people were on the ground, looking up at the tree. People want different things; not everyone wants the Truth. On this path there will never be many, because the price for the Truth is oneself, and not many are prepared to pay the whole price. Yet, as with the image of the tree which gives shelter, flowers, and fruit to all those who come, it is the job of the teacher to give people what they want.[22] A woman who was training as an opera singer once came to our group. She was with us for a year before she had to go back to New

Zealand to complete her training. I wondered what she had found during that time and just before she left she told me. She said that she had learned to let her voice sing her and not the other way round. She had found the inner security that would allow her to follow her voice, to surrender to the special gift she had been given. For her, as for the dreamer, an old driver's license had expired and been thrown away, and she had found something far more precious. And how did this happen? Whenever she had time she just came and sat in the presence of the teacher.

The Teacher Finds You

According to the Sufi tradition a teacher is necessary. But how do you find a teacher? As with many aspects of the quest, the process of finding a teacher is very different from what you might expect. You do not find a teacher; the teacher finds you. Through her aspiration and inner work the seeker lights a lamp on the inner plane. When this light is shining brightly enough it will attract the attention of a teacher with whom the seeker has a link, an inner connection. Then the teacher appears. The seeker may "just happen" to read a book or meet someone who tells her about a teacher; but such occurrences are never chance.

Often a dream will guide a seeker to the teacher. One friend who lived in New York had a dream in which she was in the green fields of England, in love with an old woman. When she awoke from this dream she still felt in love, but with whom? She was in New York, totally in love with an old lady in a dream. What was she to do? A while later she was in a bookshop when a book fell off the shelf into her hands, and she suddenly saw the old woman's face on the cover of a book. She traveled to England to meet this old woman and when she sat in front of her she just cried and cried. For years, each time she saw her she just cried.

Because the relationship with the teacher does not belong to the physical world, but to the level of the soul, it is a mysterious connection that is outside of space and time. When the moment is right, when the seeker is ready, this relationship will manifest; the teacher will be there. The teacher might live on the other side of the world or be just around the corner. The seeker might meet the teacher on this physical plane only a few times, or even never meet the teacher directly but make contact through someone who follows the same path. The seeker might spend much time in the physical presence of the teacher. Whatever is needed will be given, for it is the job of the teacher to give the seeker the best opportunity to reach Reality. For many people the physical presence of the teacher is necessary; until they have progressed far enough they need the physical presence of the teacher to make the path a living reality. For others it is the absence of the physical presence of the Teacher that makes them experience the path as an inner connection.

Physical presence or physical absence can both be necessary at different times. Each in its different way can help the seeker realize the inner nature of the real relationship with the teacher. When one friend was leaving her teacher, almost in tears because she did not know if she would ever see her again, she was told, "On this path we do not acknowledge physical separation."

At the beginning it can be necessary to be in the presence of the Teacher to make the connection "stick," to tune the vibrations of the seeker to those of the path. But human beings are so individual that for each this most important spiritual relationship will be different, and life and circumstances always give the human being what she needs at each moment. If someone is able to be in the physical presence of the teacher only once a year, he will still be given exactly what he needs. Maybe he will be given as much or more in that one meeting as others might get who sit every day in the teacher's presence. Being in the presence of the teacher is like "charging up the batteries," a process during which the seeker's attention is dynamically refocused on the goal. During our everyday life it is easy for our inner attention to wander away from the path, and during the first few years the teacher's presence can help the seeker to stay focused, and thus be able to realize his highest aspirations. After a few years the wayfarer should be so attuned to the inner vibrations of the teacher, which are the same as the vibrations of the path, that the outer, physical connection is no longer necessary.

On an outer level the teacher can be a useful figure, helping to guide the seeker through the difficulties that are encountered in day-to-day life. It is not easy to live in the world and follow a spiritual path. To have someone who is one step further along the path can be a great help. Although the teacher rarely offers direct advice, he may hint at the core of a particular problem or, through the process of reflection, help the seeker to see what is actually troubling him. Problems are immensely useful, for they are the rungs of the ladder by which we are able to ascend. Yet there are particular problems encountered on the spiritual path that can be very confusing, and the teacher may help the seeker find the best way to untangle these knots.

Sometimes guidance is given in private conversation, particularly if the problem has to do with personal relationships. However, as often as possible things are discussed within the group. Bahâ ad-dîn Naqshband said:

> Our way is that of group discussion. In solitude there is renown and in renown there is peril. Welfare is to be found in a group. Those who follow this way find great benefit and blessing in group meetings.[23]

If problems are discussed in a group they are shared in the light of the sun and their burden is lessened. One can learn from another's experiences and difficulties. Sometimes direct guidance is given by the teacher; at other times he will "speak to the door that the wall might hear." He will say something to one person that is meant for another. In this way the wayfarer learns to be always alert, always ready to catch the hint. In learning to catch the hint from the teacher, the wayfarer will learn to catch the hint from God, which is quicker than lightning. Also, however it may appear, every situation in the group is a teaching situation. Thus the wayfarer has to learn to be watchful and receptive, to distinguish between appearance and the real teaching which is often hidden beneath group discussion or even seemingly mundane conversation.

The teacher always wants the best for the wayfarer, just as a parent wants the best for a child. But the teacher can only give as much as the seeker is able to receive. In this sense it is the capacity of the seeker to take what the teacher offers that is most important. Just as the teacher is an empty space filled with the

Absolute, the seeker must aspire to be an empty space before the teacher. The more the seeker aspires and works upon himself, clearing away psychological problems and lessening the hold of the ego and the mind, the more he can be given.

MERGING WITH THE TEACHER

The teacher is necessary as a connecting link with the Absolute:

> God is nowhere. God can only be known through the Master. If you are being merged into the Teacher, you will know God. Only the Teacher is important for you. Only the Teacher. The Divine Master is complete in every way. By simply becoming like him one becomes complete in every way.[24]

The Absolute can be compared to a power station, which if it were plugged into the household electrical supply would blow every fuse. The teacher is the transformer, transforming millions of volts into the one or two hundred necessary for individual use. Through the teacher the seeker can connect with the energy of the Absolute—through merging with the teacher he can merge into the Absolute.

Sitting in the presence of the teacher helps the seeker to tune into the higher vibrations of the Self. However, the real process of spiritual transformation does not take place on the physical plane; it takes place on the level of the Self. It is here that the real teaching takes place. At this level the teaching is imprinted into the wayfarer; the dynamic energy of the guide impresses itself into the wayfarer. In the Naqshbandi Sufi system the spiritual nature and dynamism of the teacher are imprinted at the level of the Self and then reflected into ordinary consciousness. (*"Naqshband"* means in Persian "the impressor" or "the engraver," coming from the Arabic root *nqsh*: to imprint, impress, or engrave.) The Self exists within the "heart of hearts"; thus this process of teaching can be understood as a "reflection from heart to heart": the Higher Self of the teacher is reflected into the Higher Self of the wayfarer.

At its deepest level this teaching is about merging, for this is the essence of the mystic's relationship with the Absolute. The mystic longs to be so merged with the Beloved that only the Beloved exists; in the final stages he is so absorbed in the Beloved that he does not even know it:

> "The first time I entered the Holy House," stated Bâyezîd Bistâmî, "I saw the Holy House. The second time I entered it, I saw the Lord of the House. The third time I saw neither the House nor the Lord of the House."
>
> By this Bâyezîd meant, "I became lost in God, so that I knew nothing. Had I seen at all, I would have seen God." Proof of this interpretation is given by the following anecdote.
>
> A man came to the door of Bâyezîd and called out.
>
> "Whom are you seeking?" asked Bâyezîd.
>
> "Bâyezîd," replied the man.
>
> "Poor wretch!" said Bâyezîd. "I have been seeking Bâyezîd for thirty years, and cannot find any trace or token of him."[25]

Losing oneself in God is the process of *fanâ*, of annihilation. As the seeker dissolves, so the presence of the Beloved becomes greater and greater. So long as some duality remains there can be consciousness of His presence. But consciousness necessitates duality—a separation of subject and object. In states of total oneness there is neither subject nor object. When the lover is completely annihilated there is no longer any awareness; there is no longer any mirror in which His face can be seen reflected:

> Neither am I aware of being a lover, nor of love,
> Neither of my self, nor of the beloved.[26]

Such complete annihilation is the goal of the lover: to be so lost that nothing remains. This is the stamp of the real master, who can be either living or dead. Through the relationship with such a teacher the seeker receives that same imprint within the core of his being and slowly he learns to merge into it. It is through merging within the emptiness of the teacher that one realizes one's own nothingness. Bahâ ad-dîn Naqshband describes how his inner relationship with al-Hakîm at-Tirmidhî, who lived five centuries before him, had this effect:

> Twenty-two years I have been following in the footsteps of at-Tirmidhî. He had no feature and now I have no feature. Those who know will know and those who understand will understand.[27]

Even if the physical teacher has not reached this state of total annihilation, he will carry within himself this imprint—the imprint of his teacher and the imprint of the whole lineage as it stretches back to the Prophet. This great succession of masters is itself merged together in the imprint of the path. When the seeker is ready and has been tested to see if he is fully committed, then this imprint is engraved upon his heart—engraved in fire, a fire that is felt as burning longing. The essence of the path is to merge within the heart so that the imprint will burn away the lover until the veils of separation are consumed.

The relationship with the teacher takes place within the heart and it is in the heart that the whole process of merging takes place. The heart of the seeker is united with the heart of the teacher and in these moments separation dissolves. This inner experience, which takes place far beyond the conscious mind, is a gift. Through the practice of *dhikr* and meditation the wayfarer is able to realize the potential of this gift and bring it closer to consciousness. Through these practices the wayfarer inwardly aligns his whole being with the energy of the path, and empties himself of everything except the remembrance of God. The wayfarer aligns himself with the imprint hidden within the heart, and creates a container that allows this imprint to impress itself into the structure of consciousness; a hidden secret slowly reveals itself.

At the beginning there is the duality of the wayfarer and the guide. The teacher, carrying the projection of the Higher Self, appears to be full of wisdom and able to bestow spiritual nourishment upon the hungry traveler. But in essence the external teacher, being someone who has surrendered totally to the will of the Beloved, is an empty space through which the Beloved can nourish our deepest, innermost self. This is the meaning of the idea that the teacher is there to give the people what they want. Like the tree that gives shelter as well as flowers and fruit, the teacher responds to the spiritual need of the seeker, and not everyone wants the whole truth. In the following dream the teacher seems to give to everyone but the dreamer:

> I'm in an empty swimming pool. The Teacher is on the edge at one end. A friend in the group has just been to see the Teacher, and looking down from the edge of the pool greets me radiantly.
>
> "She has given me peace and stillness," she says. I feel resentful. I know many people have gone back and forth and been given something by the teacher. But not me.
>
> I walk slowly and heavily up a stairway that runs from the bottom of the pool to the top. Perhaps she will call me back. I linger, but she doesn't. I've got nothing, I say to myself. She's given me nothing. It is then I realize when I am wearily ascending the steps that I and the teacher are the same.

People get what they want, and for some a sense of peace, a touch of bliss is what they are given. But there are those for whom spiritual life is a necessity, who can never be satisfied with anything less than Absolute Truth. It is not that they are better than others, but rather that they have been imprinted, stamped long, long ago. For such people life has no meaning except as a path to the beyond. Yet this fundamental need is often coupled with a sense of abandonment, for in the deepest sense they are outcasts in this world, knowing in the depths of the heart that they belong somewhere else.

The dreamer, standing in the empty swimming pool, feels resentful. The teacher has given to everyone except her—"she has given me nothing." This is a very human feeling in a spiritual group, and is often accompanied by feelings of jealousy—others seem to progress, have wonderful dreams and experiences. We always see others more clearly than we see ourselves; our own face is the one which is most hidden from us. We are often the last to recognize our own transformation, to become aware of how much we have been given.

But the inner message of the dream touches a deeper theme. It resounds with images of emptiness, of nothingness: the swimming pool is empty, the dreamer repeatedly states that she has been given "nothing." "Only if the cup is empty can it be filled," only through nothingness and emptiness can we merge more fully; the less the ego is present the more complete can be the union with the teacher. In the truest sense the teacher gives "nothing," allowing us to touch our own nothingness, to become slowly absorbed "somewhere" far beyond the mind and the world of forms.

The dream ends with the dreamer "wearily ascending the steps"—an image which speaks to every wayfarer, who so often feels forsaken. But it is at this moment of despair that we give up the concepts we have carried, we put down our conditioning and also our expectations. Spiritual life is always other than what we expect, for it is an inner unfolding that is completely different from the mind and its concepts. Often our thoughts block us from realizing the real nature of the spiritual path, blind us to what is really happening. It is when the dreamer accepts that she will be given nothing that she is shown the true relationship with the teacher—"I and the teacher are the same."

As the training progresses, the sense of duality with the teacher gradually disappears until the Self of the wayfarer is united with the Self of the teacher. Although this union takes place on the inner planes, it is slowly integrated into the ordinary life of the Sufi, a process that may take many years. Finally it becomes a living conscious reality. Irina Tweedie explains how this process took place within her:

> The goal of every yoga is to lead a guided life, which is to listen to the voice of the Higher Self, which at the end of the training is the voice of the teacher. It is said in the scriptures that the soul of the disciple is united with the soul of the teacher. When my teacher, Bhai Sahib, told me that, I in my ignorance thought that my soul will disappear. Now how can that be? It doesn't happen that way. It is united with the teacher in the sense that it can receive the instruction or the orders of the teacher not as a duality, that is the teacher and me, but as direct knowledge inborn in the soul.
>
> When my teacher died I thought that he had betrayed me. He had made me give away all my possessions, all my money had been given to the poor, and he had seemingly given me nothing, no teaching, nothing, so I thought. Then, one night in the Himalayas I contacted him in deep meditation. He had no physical body anymore, he was a center of energy, but I knew it was him. It was so dramatic, such a

> revelation. I was no longer alone. He was like a big daddy. I could go into meditation and ask any question, only for others, never for myself, and receive wonderful answers. What a security it was. But gradually, very gradually, without my even noticing it, a kind of transformation happened. There was no teacher and there was. There was no teacher in the sense that I couldn't see him anymore, I couldn't contact him anymore. But when I needed, only when I needed, I knew. And my mind, now used to this process of gradual absorption, knew that it is not me, not Tweedie. One minute before I didn't know the answer. Something else within me which is united with the teacher knew.[28]

Light upon Light

The wayfarer merges into the teacher who in turn is merged into the Beloved. In essence there is neither wayfarer and teacher, nor lover and Beloved—only one light revealing itself. This revelation happens within the heart, which is the meeting place of the wayfarer, the teacher, and the Beloved. Within the heart He calls to Himself: light calls to light; light evokes light; light merges into light. The more completely the wayfarer merges within the heart, the deeper he is immersed in this process. In the following dream the final image is just light:

> I enter my teacher's courtyard and see him sitting on the other side, using his mala [a kind of rosary], which he is immersing in a bowl of

> water. I come to him and look into the bowl, but instead of seeing either my face, the teacher's hand, or the mala, I just see light.

With the beads of the mala moving through his fingers, the teacher prays. The deepest prayer is without words; it is a silent merging into the emptiness which is the fullness of God. As the teacher immerses himself in prayer, the wayfarer too is a part of that prayer, for the merging of the teacher is reflected into the heart of the wayfarer. Looking into the bowl, the dreamer sees the true nature of this reflection. There is not her face, nor the teacher's hand, nor the mala. There is only light. In the words of the Christian mystic, The Blessed John Ruysbroeck,

> Here there is nothing but an eternal seeing and staring at that Light, by that Light, and in that Light.[29]

THE POVERTY OF THE HEART

Last night my teacher taught me the lesson of Poverty:
Having nothing and wanting nothing.

Rûmî[1]

The Sackcloth Coat of Poverty

The Sufi path takes the wayfarer beyond the world of forms into the formless, beyond the mind into the heart. On this journey every desire is a limitation:

> An intending disciple said to Dhû-l-Nûn, the Egyptian: "Above everything in this world I wish to enroll in the Path of Truth."
>
> Dhû-l-Nûn told him: "You can accompany our caravan only if you first accept two things. One is that you will have to do things which you do not want to do. The other is that you will not be permitted to do things which you desire to do. It is 'wanting' which stands between man and the Path of Truth."[2]

Those who travel along this path are known in the East as "dervishes" *(darwish* in modern Persian), a term which refers to their holy poverty; to quote Hujwîrî, "The poor man is not he whose hand is empty of provisions, but he whose nature is empty of desires." Poverty is an essential quality for the wayfarer, the poverty of the heart which embraces every aspect of his life and leads to a lover's state of absolute inner dependence upon his Beloved.

Poverty is a state of both helplessness and freedom, in which the wayfarer, without desire or direction, has nothing and nowhere to go. Such total poverty is the real patched coat of the Sufi:

> A dervish wearing a sackcloth coat and woolen cap once came to meet Master Abû 'Alî. One of Abû 'Alî's disciples tried to humor him, saying, "How much did you purchase that sackcloth for?"
>
> The dervish answered, "I purchased it for the sum of the world. I was offered the hereafter in exchange, but refused to trade."

Ultimately, if everything must be given up, even the desire for spiritual progress is a limitation. The road which seemed to lead to a far distant horizon is seen as just another illusion. For the seeker who has followed the path of his longings and placed all his values in the idea of the quest, it can be very hard to give up this spiritual attachment. But not only must this world be given up; any idea of spiritual transformation must also be abandoned.

Spiritual poverty is to be totally naked, to be a formless piece of wax in which He can stamp His name. Because this state is beyond desire, poverty cannot be sought. Like everything that belongs to Him, it is given as a gift. The path takes the wayfarer to where he can travel no further and is left in a state of desolation and hopelessness. Then, when the seeker accepts there is nowhere else to go—when the path seems to lead to a total dead end—then there is freedom, freedom born from the deep realization that there is nothing one can do. It is in this new-found emptiness that spiritual life really begins.

THE DUSTY PATH

The journey that takes the seeker to the end of the road is hard and painful. It is a journey that sometimes leads away from the sunshine of the world into the darkness of our inner being. The following dream describes this journey. It images a process that took many years and much suffering but led the dreamer beyond the ego to the ocean of the Self:

> I was walking along a dirt road which stretched parallel to a main, paved road. The paved road was on my right and further over there were yellow fields and blue, open skies. It was bright and sunny on that side. To the left of the dirt road was a forest, dark and shady.
>
> As I was walking I saw on my left a huge tree. It was standing out from all the rest of the trees in the forest. Its trunk was wide and its branches stretched out far and were themselves so long that they were bending towards the ground. They were very thick and full of leaves. Then I noticed the roots of the tree, the parts of which were exposed. They too were thick and abundant, twisting like huge sinews.
>
> I felt a tremendous pull to enter this tree. Where the branches were bending down there seemed to be an opening. At the same time I knew that this meant leaving the sunny, open spaces and part of me was reluctant to do this. There was a split second of hesitation. Finally, I let myself go. As I entered through the opening I had to bend because the branches were so low. Then, as I went further in I had to bend even more, because the branches became lower and

> lower and closer and closer to me. I felt them around my body, really wrapping me over, and then I had to crawl on the ground because there was no space to walk, even bent. As I was crawling the branches were wrapping me even more.
>
> "Soon I won't be able to move," I was thinking. "I'll have to stay where I am, frozen and immobile." This was not an alarming thought, it was just an evaluation of the situation. I also thought that now I would become a pupa, with all these layers of leaves and branches wrapping me over. Then I felt that I was gliding, as if something was gently pushing me forward. I completely let myself go and enjoyed the feeling of surrendering to whatever was doing the gliding for me.
>
> Soon enough I was on the other side of the forest and there in front of me was the sea. It was at sunset or dawn, with pinkish-gold light, as in a Turner painting. Into the mirror-calm sea a river was flowing from the right, wide and calm yet definitely moving. I just gazed, wondering, "After all it was not that difficult."

In this sequence of symbolic images this dream tells half a lifetime's story. It begins with the dreamer walking on a dirt road beside a main, paved road. The Sufi traveler does not walk along the world's main road; his is a dustier path. "Be in this world as if you are a traveler," goes a saying ascribed to the Prophet, "a passerby, with your clothes and shoes full of dust. Sometimes you sit under the shade of a tree, sometimes you walk in the desert. Be always a passerby, for this is not home."[3]

The main road is on the dreamer's right and further on are fields and blue skies. The right-hand side symbolizes consciousness, where the sun shines clear and bright. But the Sufi path includes the dust and dirt of the unconscious, where life is neither clear nor paved. On the left side of this dirt road lies the forest, "dark and shady," imaging the primordial world of the unconscious. Standing out of the forest, close to the unconscious, is a huge tree. The tree is one of the great archetypal symbols. It is the tree of life, the world tree which stands on the axis of the world, the *axis mundi.* Drawing water from the very depths of the earth, it gives nourishment and shelter to all life. Yet, at the same time, the world tree is not other than ourselves. It is our own being which is rooted in the center of the cosmos. Joseph Campbell describes how the *axis mundi* is

> the central point, the pole around which all revolves. The central point of the world is the point where stillness and movement are together. Movement is time, but stillness is eternity. Realizing how this moment of your life is actually a moment of eternity, and experiencing the eternal aspect of what you're doing in the temporal experience—this is the mythological experience.[4]

The tree of life is one's inner axis that grows from the depths of the earth and reaches to the heavens. It connects the primal opposites of the temporal and the eternal. It is life lived from the "still center of the turning world" and it embraces the deepest human mystery: that we are eternal beings living in a world of time.

The dreamer feels a tremendous pull to enter this tree. The spiritual path always takes us back to the center of ourselves—not to the little conscious ego but to the depths and glory of our real being. At first, as one walks the dusty path of the spiritual traveler, there is usually a sense of conscious direction. Seeking a spiritual goal or ideal, an individual often follows the codes or ideas of a specific spiritual tradition. She practices a certain meditation or other spiritual exercises, and may read some of the sacred texts. But there comes the time when the seeker feels a pull that takes her away from any conscious path, a pull that is the call of her own inner nature, that takes her from the known world into the unknown depths of herself. Then the sunlight is left behind and the unconscious takes us into itself, for it is always in the depths of our own being that the transformation takes place.

From the River to the Sea

The dreamer feels a moment's hesitation about leaving the "sunny, open spaces," but then she lets herself go. One cannot overstate the importance of just letting oneself go. At the core of the Sufi path are the practice of surrender and the necessity of having faith and trusting a system that will totally transform you. Like lovers we have to allow ourselves to be taken—first into the darkness of the unconscious and then later into the dazzling darkness that is the formlessness of God, "the dark silence in which all lovers lose themselves."[5]

As the dreamer enters the tree which is her own inner self, she has to bend low and then bend even more as the branches become lower and lower. The greatest teacher of humility is our own shadow—the cruelty, the pettiness, the anger and resentment that we find within us. The deeper we travel within ourselves, the more we are shown our own inadequacies, our own failures. Finally, we are taken to the point where we realize that we can no longer make this journey, that we can do nothing, that we can go no further. We have given everything to achieve our goal; yet we cannot reach it. This often manifests on the psychological level as a problem which we are totally unable to resolve. We have tried everything and it is still beyond us. It has demanded everything; it has pushed us to our own limits and past them. This is often the moment of deepest despair. We are confronted with our own limitation and all that is left is the call for help from the depths of the heart. In this way we are driven to surrender.

In this process it is important that we have totally committed ourselves and tried our utmost; otherwise the surrender will not be complete. It is only when we have fully experienced our own effort that we can feel its inadequacy. Then we have no other option but to give up. This surrender is most painful, for it involves the death of the ego.

Once the ego steps out of the way, something else can take over. Our dreamer had been pushed by painful inner and outer circumstances to the point where her ego could no longer even attempt to determine her actions. Pushed lower and lower by the branches, she is forced to crawl and then realizes that "Soon I won't be able to move.... I'll just have to stay where I am, frozen, immobile." But it is at this point of inner inaction, which she does not resist but accepts, that the transformation begins. First she has the image of herself as a "pupa," the chrysalis from which the butterfly of the soul will be born. Then she feels herself gliding forward and letting go, surrendering to a force that is greater than her ego.

Once we are surrendered and no longer struggling to determine our own direction, then spiritual life becomes easier. We cease to resist the energies of the Higher Self and thus are able to experience our individual life as a part of the universal sea of our deeper existence. This is the final image of the dream, when the dreamer leaves the forest of the unconscious to glimpse the inner world of the Self. In front of the dreamer is the sea, "at sunset or dawn, with pinkish-gold light." The beauty of the scene and its quality of light suggest a level of consciousness beyond the ego. In this higher dimension there is neither trouble nor turbulence, for the sea is mirror-calm, and into this universal sea flows the river of the dreamer's own individual life. She gazes, wondering, for this inner reality can evoke only awe and wonder.

The dream's final statement, "after all it was not that difficult," reflects the fact that difficulties are only born of resistance. Once one has given up, the energies of transformation can flow freely. The darkness of despair is only a passing stage that takes one to the point of acknowledging one's own poverty. Yet the paradox of spiritual life is that this poverty is infinitely valuable, for it opens the door to the Beyond: "Blessed are the poor in spirit: for theirs is the kingdom of heaven."[6]

The Narrow Uphill Path

Each in our own way, we are faced with difficulties that are too great for us to overcome. We struggle and are defeated again and again, until finally we fully accept our defeat. Just as a horse must be broken before it can be ridden, so is the seeker "broken" so that Another can take the reins of her life. In another friend's dream, as the dreamer drives uphill, the way becomes more and more difficult:

> I am in a white car, driving along a road. It is raining very heavily and the road goes uphill getting narrower and narrower. There is a landslide and it is very difficult to drive. I have to hold the wheel with both hands and slowly drive through the rain. Then I get to the top and park the car. I get out and there is a shadowy figure beside me, very large.

At the beginning the spiritual path is an uphill struggle, demanding every ounce of effort we have to give. The road gets "narrower and narrower," for this path is "as narrow as the edge of a razor": "strait is the gate, and narrow is the way which leadeth unto life, and few there be that find it."[7] The spiritual path demands that the wayfarer keep her attention fixed on the goal, for only then can the spiritual dimension begin to manifest within. This inner focus is the channel through which the transformative energies of the soul enter our ordinary consciousness; it forms a link between the ego and the Self. At the beginning every effort is needed to keep open this channel, to hold the thread, which is so easily lost amid the many distractions of both the outer world and the world of the unconscious. The dreamer must hold the wheel of her car "with both hands," suggesting a maximized attention with both the right and the left side, the masculine and feminine in balance.

In the dream it is "raining heavily" which makes the drive more difficult, even causing a landslide. Rain is often symbolic of grace, falling from above to below. One of the paradoxes of the path is that at the beginning the spiritual influences are often confusing and appear to make the journey more difficult. Similarly, the teacher will seem to put obstacles in the way of the seeker, will seem to be confusing and contradicting. This is because the spiritual reality is so different from that of our ordinary consciousness that in order for us to experience this inner reality, the patterns of worldly conditioning need to be broken. Spiritual truth appears so contradictory to our logical mind that it is often expressed in paradoxes, which confuse our normal patterns of thought. To quote Aristides: "And it is in fact the paradox which is the highest thing in the gods' cures." In the dream the image of the landslide reflects the way this inner dynamic makes everything unstable, for only through insecurity can the real inner security be reached.

Despite the difficulties, the dreamer reaches the top of the hill. There she parks the car and gets out. She sees beside her a "very large" shadowy figure. The dreamer associated this figure with the teacher, who was shadowy because he was as yet indistinct. His presence suggests symbolically that she has now made a relationship with her Higher Self. Her inner effort and total attention have achieved their result. She has forged this inner link but now her white car, imaging this sense of inner purpose, must be left behind. It is a vehicle that has served its purpose, but on the next stage of the journey any sense of direction, any struggle towards the goal, is a limitation. The next stage is a total surrender to the Higher Self, a state of spiritual poverty as described by Meister Eckhart:

> A man must become truly poor and free from his creaturely will as he was when he was born. And I tell you, by the Eternal Truth, that so long as you desire to fulfill the will of God and have any hankering after eternity and God, for just so long you are not truly poor. He alone has spiritual poverty who wills nothing, knows nothing, desires nothing.[8]

This state of poverty is an attitude of commitment in which the whole being of the wayfarer is surrendered to the path so that the path and the wayfarer are one. Because there is no longer any duality between the path and the traveler, there is nowhere to go—except to stay surrendered. Empty of direction, the Sufi can then become an instrument in the hands of the One—can be His slave, working in the world as He wills.

Turning Back to the World

On the first stage of the journey the traveler turns her attention from the outer world, returning within to find the source of her individual life. This source is the rock of the Self from which life flows. But in order to complete the journey, the traveler must turn back to the world. No longer isolated by the desires of the ego, she lives life as an integral part of the unfolding whole. Then she experiences the river of life as springing from the source and flowing into the ocean of the Self. The seeker knows from where she has come and where she is going; she knows the beginning and the end, alpha and omega, as one. This process of turning back to the river of life is imaged in a subsequent dream of the woman who dreamt of the journey up the steep and narrowing road:

> I was walking up a huge rocky mountain which had many waterfalls. At one point I looked above me and saw a group of children jumping into a waterfall. I was watching them play from below. When I got to the waterfall one of the children dropped into my arms. I just stood there and contemplated his beauty.
>
> I continued walking up the mountain alone. In the distance I saw the teacher sitting on a rock. Her back was to me and she was wearing a black dress. Facing her was a woman about my age who was in a meditative state, with her eyes closed. As I got closer I could see that the teacher was reading a book with nothing written in it. As I stood next to her at the edge of a cliff, I could see a huge cascade on the right, with pure, clear water which was very deep. The water was running down the mountain with tremendous force. I don't know whether the teacher pushed me or I fell but I saw myself disappearing into the depths of the cascading water.

Again there is the image of ascending, though this time the dreamer is on foot. In contrast to the traveler's ascent is the image of water falling. "If you walk toward Him, He comes to you running." The grace of God comes to meet the wayfarer but now it does not appear to make the journey more difficult. Instead the children play in a waterfall; this suggests an innocent and joyful relationship between the dreamer and the pure essence of life that falls from above. Christ's words, "Suffer little children, and forbid them not, to come unto me: for of such is the kingdom of heaven," reflect the innocence of our essential nature.[9] This is the simplicity and beauty of life that is lived close to the source and which sadly we have almost lost in our sophisticated world. To return to the Self is to return to this inner child, as Blake movingly images in one of his *Songs of Innocence:*

> When the voices of children are heard on the green
> And laughing is heard on the hill,
> My heart is at rest within my breast,
> And everything else is still.[10]

When the dreamer arrives at the waterfall she finds one of these children has "dropped into my arms." The innocence and purity of her own nature are given back to her and she can only "contemplate" its beauty. This inner child is a dynamic state of being. It is the flow of life itself in which the inner qualities of beauty are made visible. Just as a flower opens to the sun, so does our true beauty become visible in the light of the Self. It effortlessly radiates its nature into our everyday life. This is the inner meaning of Christ's saying:

> Consider the lilies of the field, how they grow; they toil not, neither do they spin.
>
> And yet I say unto you, That even Solomon in all his glory was not arrayed like one of these.[11]

The Witness and the Teacher

After experiencing the beauty of her inner child, the dreamer continues up the mountain, alone. True inner poverty is total non-attachment; everything must be left behind. Then the dreamer sees the teacher sitting on a rock, which is a symbol of the bare essence which is the Self. The Self has many aspects: innocence, purity, beauty, and bliss. The Self also has a quality of barrenness, as empty as a desert, as bare as a rock. The teacher's back is towards the dreamer and she is wearing black. Black is no color; it represents "mystical poverty," a state of total annihilation in God.

The teacher, dressed in black, images the ultimate stage of spiritual poverty—*fâna*, complete annihilation in God, a state of total nothingness.[12] Although this state of annihilation exists as a potential within the dreamer, it is not yet known to her; she can only see the teacher's back. However, facing the teacher is a "woman about my age who was in a meditative state, with her eyes closed." This figure is reminiscent of Jung's dream of a yogi sitting in deep meditation. This yogi had Jung's face; and Jung awoke from the dream with the thought, "Aha, so he is the one who is meditating me. He has a dream, and I am it."[13]

The meditating yogi images Jung's Higher Self, what the Sufis refer to as the "witness in heaven" *(shâhid fi'l- samâ)*. It is through the witness that God contemplates the beauty of His creation. Just as the dreamer contemplates the beauty of her inner child, so does the Beloved contemplate the beauty of His child, the lover, through the eyes of the lover's Higher Self, the witness. Furthermore, just as our shadow, our inner darkness, separates us from the beauty of our own essential nature, so does this same darkness fall like veils between the Beloved and the lover. In climbing the uphill path the seeker is working on the shadow, removing the veils of darkness. When the veils are removed the Beloved sees the face of His lover; through the eyes of the witness He realizes His own beauty.

The relationship between the lover and the Beloved has a two-way dynamic in which the witness is an intermediary. The beauty of the Beloved is such that the lover would be blinded by even a glimpse; yet the lover can come to know the witness, the "Inner Man of Light." The Sufi saying, "He who knows himself, knows his Lord," refers to the fact that through self-knowledge the seeker comes to know his Higher Self, "his Lord." The Higher Self is the part of our being which has never become separate from the Source. It is one with God; this is what Christ meant when, speaking from the level of the Self, he said; "I and my Father are one."[14]

By forging the link with the Higher Self, not only does the lover come to know her own divinity but she also allows the Beloved to know His creation. In this way the lover fulfills the deepest purpose of creation: He who is alone and perfect created the universe in order that He might know Himself. Spiritual poverty is the state of inner emptiness or purity of heart that is necessary for the Beloved to experience Himself undistorted; only in the pure, unblemished mirror of the heart can the Beloved see His own face. The basis of any mystical experience is that the lover is a vehicle through which the Beloved can come to know Himself. The whole being of the lover, even the very cells of the body, participate in this "Self-Knowing." The greater this state of spiritual poverty—the more complete the annihilation of the lover—the greater is this participation.

Poverty Imprinted in the Heart

In the dream, the woman who is meditating sits facing the teacher. This image points towards the essence of the teacher-wayfarer relationship, which takes place on the level of the Higher Self. At this level the teacher makes the wayfarer like herself: the spiritual poverty of the teacher is impressed into the heart of the wayfarer. But in order for this inner process to be realized, the wayfarer must work in the world as God's slave. This relationship between the inner teaching and the outer work is an essential aspect of the Sufi path, for it is the combination of the inner secrets and the ordinary everyday world that makes the path a dynamic living reality within the wayfarer. The most sublime and the most ordinary are fused together in the selfless service of the Sufi; the "highest" and "lowest" are brought together and nothing is excluded. The full potential of the human being is in our belonging to both the world of spirit and the world of matter. In embracing these polarities the wayfarer can realize this potential: "Correctly combined, the secrets and the most ordinary things in this life may make it possible to achieve the Longest Journey."[15]

Moreover, the inner teaching is never given for oneself. It is always for others. Through service a link is formed between the inner dimension of the Self and the outer world of consciousness. The energies of the spiritual dimensions can enter into the outer world without being obstructed by the ego. Spiritual poverty is therefore a state of inner emptiness and outer service, as is movingly expressed by Mother Teresa:

> I don't claim anything of the work. I am a little pencil in His Hand. That is all. He does the thinking. He does the writing. The pencil has nothing to do with it.[16]

The Empty Book

In the dream the teacher is "reading a book with nothing written in it." This book is the book of life and its emptiness again images a state of spiritual poverty. The pages of our book of life are normally filled with the actions of the ego. In a state of poverty these pages are empty, for the Sufi no longer enacts the will of the ego but lives in a state of unknowing:

> Do you think I know what I'm doing?
> That for one breath or half a breath
> I belong to myself?
> As much as a pen knows what it's writing,
> or the ball can guess where it's going next.[17]

These words by Rûmî, like those of Mother Teresa, describe the mystical state of absorption in which the consciousness of the mystic is lost in that of God. The mystic no longer exists; only He is. This "empty book" is a latent reality within the dreamer. It is an inner state of being, which, reflected from the teacher, will manifest within her heart in the process of service.

The dreamer's journey began with climbing the mountain, suggesting a period of introversion as she turned her attention away from the outer world to establish a connection with the Self. But the challenge is then to live in the world and remain centered in the Self. This is the stage that the alchemists called the *rubedo*, the reddening. Only by being lived out does an inner state become fully realized. Spiritual life must be lived in the world, in the marketplace. And for the Sufi the friction between the inner states and the pressures of outer life energizes the process of transformation. All energy is born from the tension of opposites, and even mundane experiences like financial worries force one to make an effort to try to reconcile the inner and outer realities. Here lies the secret alchemy of the Sufi path:

> We have to live our life in the world and be occupied with worldly affairs, and reach the highest stage in spite, or rather, because of it. For the greater is the limitation, the greater will be the ultimate perfection by overcoming it.[18]

The traveler on the spiritual path is continually thrown between the opposites. Contraction is followed by expansion; the out-breath follows the in-breath. After climbing the mountain the dreamer must return to the valley, must make the journey from the source along the river of life till it reaches the ocean. On the right side of the dreamer falls a huge cascade of "pure, clear water." This is the water of life which flows from the source, the same water that St. John saw in his vision: "And he shewed me a pure river of water of life, clear as crystal, proceeding out of the Throne of God and of the Lamb."[19] This river flows from within us, is our own pure essence manifesting itself. Through service this water flows into the world, purifying and cleansing others. The Sufi performs his outer duties in the world while his inner attention remains focused on the source. Simply through keeping this connection between the inner essence and the outer world, the Sufi allows the higher energies of the Beyond to heal and transform life.

The period of introversion, of turning inward to find what was hidden and to reconnect with the Self, is followed by turning back to the world. In the Naqshbandi Sufi tradition, the wayfarer is sent, or thrown, back into the world when he or she is ready. Only the teacher knows this moment:

> I send my people away, as soon as the Training is finished. Now go and work, I say, and they go. My people are tested with Fire and Spirit, and then sent out into the world, and never, never do they go wrong.[20]

Sometimes a new "work opportunity" will unexpectedly present itself to the wayfarer. Sometimes this return to the world is simply a change of inner focus, away from introspection into a fuller involvement with outer affairs. There is often a feeling that this change is not spiritual, for it appears to involve a loss of attention to inner aspirations. One friend was very disturbed by the fact that his suddenly increased work load involved such a degree of mental attention (he was working with computers and other machines) that he could no longer keep his conscious attention on his silent *dhikr*. But on this path we are not even attached to our spiritual practices. Every attachment is a barrier; even spiritual ideals can become a limitation. This friend's dreams, together with the hints of the teacher, encouraged him to continue with this work, for through this process he would realize how his spiritual commitment had become part of his whole being. It is said, "First you do the *dhikr*, then the *dhikr* does you." This friend's inner focus and aspiration had taken him to the state where the connection with his Higher Self was secure and dynamic enough to work on its own. The Higher Self could now manifest in his ordinary, everyday life. But in order to realize this he had to give up his conscious spiritual attitudes; only then would he realize how his whole inner being was walking the path home.

We easily form attachments and on the path any attachment is a limitation. Even the concept of spiritual life with its focus on inner aspiration can itself become a form of security that must be surrendered. To free ourselves may require a shock, or a push back into the marketplace of the world. Our dreamer did not know whether she was pushed by the teacher or fell into the waterfall. She only saw herself "disappearing into the depths of the cascading water," for it is in the depths of life that the annihilation of the wayfarer takes place: in service we forget ourselves. This service carries the stamp of poverty: we want nothing, and even to want to help another creates a limitation and a barrier.

From this state of self-forgetfulness, mystical poverty becomes a living reality. The opposites of the inner and outer worlds fuse together and are contained within the heart. The lover has fully abandoned both his inner and outer life to the Beloved and has become an "inert thing" in His hands. St. Catherine of Genoa, who combined a life of service (organizing and administering her hospitals) with that of a contemplative lover, described such a state of total poverty:

> Since Love took charge of everything, I have not taken care of anything, and I have never been able to work with my intellect, memory and will, any more than if I never had them. Indeed every day I feel myself more occupied in Him, and with greater fire.... If I spoke of the spiritual things that often beset me, at once my Love would reprove me, saying that I ought not to speak but let myself wholly burn, without attempting any word or act to bring relief to soul or body. If I was silent and took no heed of anything, but simply said: "If the body is dying, let it die. If it can't carry on, let it be. Nothing matters to me," then Love would still reprove me saying: "I want you to shut your eyes tight so that you see nothing of the work that I am doing in you as if it were in you. I want you to be dead, and every sight however perfect annihilated in you. I do not want you to do anything which may be of yourself."
>
> When I had locked my mouth and stood like an inert thing from Love's tightening grasp within me, I felt such interior peace and contentment that I was unsupportable to myself.[21]

The mystical path takes the traveler to a state of abandonment that is so total it cannot even be understood. All that can be said with certainty is: "I know nothing, I understand nothing, I am unaware of myself.

I am in love, but with whom I do not know. My heart is at the same time both full and empty of love."[22] This state of unknowingness is fundamental to all mystics, to all those whom love has emptied. We must be nothing and nowhere, so lost that there is nothing left to find. In the words of a Sufi master, "There is nothing but Nothingness."[23] By our own efforts we cannot reach this Ultimate Nothingness, but through poverty we can be taken there—through poverty we can become Nothing.

> There was a king, who, one day, entering his royal court, observed one person, who among all those present was not bowing down before him. Unnerved by the impudent act of this stranger in the hall, the king called out: "How dare you not bow down before me! Only God does not bow down before me, and there is nothing greater than God. Who then are you?" The tattered stranger answered with a smile, "I am that nothing."[24]

NOTES

Notes to the Introduction

1. Irina Tweedie, unpublished quotation.

The Fools of God

1. Rûmî, quoted by Miriam and Jose Arguelles in *The Feminine*, p. 123.
2. Farîd ud-Dîn 'Attâr, *The Conference of the Birds*, trans. C. S. Nott, ch. 39 ("The Valley of Love").
3. Shakespeare, *Hamlet*, II.ii. 249-250.
4. 'Attâr, *The Conference of the Birds*, ch. 39 ("An Arab in Persia").
5. *St. John*, 6:63. Compare with Irina Tweedie's teacher, Bhai Sahib: "We do not teach—we quicken." Irina Tweedie, *Daughter of Fire*, p. 219.
6. T. S. Eliot, "Burnt Norton," ll. 42-43.
7. Quoted by Irina Tweedie: "Sufi spiritual training is a process of individuation leading to the Infinite," in *Sufism, Islam and Jungian Psychology*, ed. J. Marvin Spiegelman, pp. 127-128.
8. Quoted by Jâmî in *The Abode of Spring*, abridged and translated by David Pendlebury, in *Four Sufi Classics*, p. 192.
9. Qur'an 18:61-82, trans. N. J. Dawood, slightly adapted. Subsequent quotations from the Qur'an are from Dawood unless stated otherwise.

Khidr, the Green Man, is an important Sufi figure who represents the direct revelation of Divine Truth. He is described in this passage in the Qur'an as "one of Our servants to whom We had vouchsafed Our mercy and whom We had endowed with knowledge of Our Own." See also C. G. Jung, *Collected Works,* vol. 9i, para. 243-258, for his psychological interpretation of this story.

10. Irina Tweedie, *Daughter of Fire*, p. 149.
11. Quoted by R. A. Nicholson in *The Mystics of Islam*, p. 115.
12. Tweedie, p. 323.
13. Quoted by Cyprian Rice in *The Persian Sufis*, p. 32.
14. For a fuller exploration of the symbolism of the tree of life, see pp. 245-246 below. It is referred to as "the pole around which all revolves," a description which is also used of Khidr: "I am the unique Pole that is the sum of all" ('Abd al-Karîm Jîlî, quoted by Henry Corbin in *Spiritual Body and Celestial Earth*, p. 157).
15. Quoted by Corbin in *The Man of Light in Iranian Sufism*, p. 34.
16. Tweedie, unpublished quotation.
17. Sermon: "Blessed are the Poor."
18. Corbin, referring to Sohravardî's *Recital of the Occidental Exile*, in *The Man of Light in Iranian Sufism*, p. 43.
19. 'Abd al-Karîm Jîlî, quoted by Corbin in *Spiritual Body and Celestial Earth*, p. 156.
20. C. G. Jung, *C. G. Jung, Emma Jung, and Toni Wolff: A Collection of Remembrances*, ed. Ferne Jensen, pp. 51-52.
21. 'Attâr, trans. Javad Nurbakhsh, in *Sufi Symbolism*, vol. 1, p. 75.
22. Tweedie, p. 180.
23. Ibn 'Arabî, describing our relationship with the divine aspect of the feminine, quoted by Henry Corbin in *Creative Imagination in the Sufism of Ibn 'Arabi*, p. 174. For the full text of this passage see below, pp. 143-145.
24. Qur'an 24:41, quoted by Corbin in *Creative Imagination in the Sufism of Ibn 'Arabi*, pp. 109-110.
25. Tweedie, p. 793.
26. Tweedie, p. 200.
27. Nancy Qualls-Corbett, *The Sacred Prostitute*, p. 62.
28. *St. Matthew*, 6:21-29. See also p. 252 below.
29. Quoted by Rice, p. 76.
30. The daughter carries her father's anima projection only too often. It usually happens when either he has a difficult relationship with his wife, or his wife carries his

mother image. The danger is that this anima projection will lead to an emotionally (or possibly physically) incestuous relationship between father and daughter. The mother-son relationship carries the possibility of having a similar dynamic, particularly when a mother is a single parent.

31. Bibi Hayati, "Before there was a trace of this world of men," trans. Jane Hirshfield, *The Enlightened Heart*, ed. Stephen Mitchell, p. 107.

32. Quoted by Nicholson, *The Mystics of Islam*, p. 68.

33. Rûmî, "A Thief in the Night," trans. Peter Lamborn Wilson and Nasrollah Pourjavady in *The Drunken Universe*, p. 105.

The Feminine Side of Love

1. "The source of my grief and loneliness is deep in my breast," trans. Charles Upton, *Doorkeeper of the Heart*, p. 34.

2. Tweedie, p. 135.

3. Farîd ud-Dîn 'Attâr, *Muslim Saints and Mystics*, trans. A. J. Arberry, pp. 93-94.

4. Francis Thompson, "The Hound of Heaven."

5. Al-Junayd, quoted by R. S. Bhatnagar, *Dimensions of Classical Sufi Thought*, pp. 171-172.

6. Quoted by R. A. Nicholson, *Studies in Islamic Mysticism*, p. 55.

7. Jung, *Collected Works*, vol. 14, para. 180.

8. *Tao Te Ching*, trans. Stephen Mitchell, ch. 15.

9. Tweedie, p. 157.

10. C. G. Jung, *Collected Letters*, vol. 1, p. 278.

11. Tweedie, p. 404.

12. *The Abode of Spring*, in *Four Sufi Classics*, p. 191.

13. Jung, *Collected Works*, vol. 16, para. 475.

The Alchemical Opus I: The Transformation of the Shadow

1. Jung, *Collected Works*, vol. 13, para. 335.
2. Tweedie, p. x.
3. Jung, *Collected Works*, vol. 7, para. 103 n.
4. Robert Bly, *A Little Book on the Human Shadow*, p. 17.
5. C. G. Jung, *The Psychology of the Transference*, p. 34.
6. *St. Matthew*, 10:34-35.
7. Jung, *Collected Works*, vol. 12, para. 434.
8. For the symbolism of green, see above, p. 15.
9. Jung, *Collected Works*, vol. 13, para. 161.
10. Psalm 118:22.
11. *The Hermetic Museum*, 1:13, quoted by Edward Edinger in *The Anatomy of the Psyche*, p. 11.
12. Marie-Louise von Franz, *C. G. Jung, His Myth in Our Time*, p. 222.
13. Jung, *Collected Works*, vol. 12, para. 433.
14. Tweedie, p. 345.
15. Jung, *C. G. Jung Speaking*, p. 229, quoted by Edinger, p. 147.
16. 'Attâr, *The Conference of the Birds*, p. 132.
17. Jung, *C. G. Jung, Emma Jung, and Toni Wolff: A Collection of Remembrances*, p. 53.
18. "Individuation" is fundamentally a natural developmental "process immanent in every living organism." It is what makes an acorn develop into an oak, a kitten into a cat. Within a human being it can occur "more or less autonomously without the participation of consciousness." But the more common understanding of the term is when it refers to an "artificial" process, which is "developed by definite methods" (for example analysis) and *"experienced consciously"* (Jolande Jacobi, *The Way of Individuation*, p. 15).
19. Sallie Nichols, *Jung and Tarot, An Archetypal Journey*, ch. 19.

The Pain of the Collective Shadow

1. Annemarie Schimmel, *Pain and Grace*, p. 192.
2. *Gitanjali*, I.1
3. Jung, *Collected Works*, vol. 12, para. 518f.
4. "As the process deepens one realizes more and more that insights come by grace and that the development occurs not by the will of the ego but by the urge to development from the Self." Edinger, p. 6.
5. J. E. Cirlot, *A Dictionary of Symbols*, p. 251.
6. William Wordsworth, "Ode: Intimations of Immortality from Recollections of Early Childhood," l. 76.
7. Wordsworth, "Intimations of Immortality," ll. 1-9.
8. M. Esther Harding, *Woman's Mysteries*, p. 103.
9. Jung, *Collected Works*, vol. 11, para. 235 n.
10. Irina Tweedie, Foreword, *The Lover and the Serpent*, p. xiii.
11. Olive Schreiner, *Dreams*, pp. 119-121.
12. Quoted in *The Abode of Spring*, in *Four Sufi Classics*, p. 191.
13. Mirabai, unknown source.
14. T. S. Eliot, "Little Gidding," ll. 239-242.
15. In reality, to stare a wild animal in the eyes is usually an aggressive act, which the animal reads as the prelude to a fight. In an encounter with a dangerous wild animal, it is best to look down and back away.
16. Jung, *Collected Works*, vol. 5, para. 267.
17. Quoted by Maynard Mack in *Shakespeare: Hamlet, A Casebook,* ed. John Jump, p. 107.
18. T. S. Eliot, "Ash Wednesday," I, l. 38.
19. Jung, *Collected Works*, vol. 6, para. 709.
20. Tweedie, p. 475.
21. *St. John*, 3:6-8.
22. Tweedie, p. 441.
23. Ghalib, trans. Jane Hirshfield, *The Enlightened Heart*, ed. Stephen Mitchell, p. 104.

The Alchemical Opus II: The Inner Partner

1. Trans. John Moyne and Coleman Barks, *Open Secret*, p. 19.
2. Jung, *Collected Works*, vol. 9ii, para. 42.
3. Jung, *Collected Works*, vol. 12, para. 219 and n.
4. Irene de Castillejo, *Knowing Woman*, p. 76.
5. Von Franz mentions four stages of development in both the animus and anima: first, the wholly physical man or woman—Tarzan, or Eve, the primitive instinctual type; second, the romantic figure—Lord Byron or Helen of Troy; third the animus, the bearer of the "word"—a professor or clergyman—and the anima, a figure of spiritual devotion—the Virgin Mary; and fourth, the animus and anima as figures of wisdom—Gandhi or the Greek goddess of wisdom, Athena *(Man and His Symbols*, ed. C. G. Jung, pp. 184 and 195).
6. Von Franz, *Man and His Symbols*, ed. Jung, p. 194.
7. Jung, *Collected Works*, vol. 14, para. 654.
8. Erich Neumann, "The Psychological Stages of Feminine Development," *Spring*, 1957, p. 72.
9. Jung, *Word and Image*, p. 211.
10. *The Book of Common Prayer*.
11. *Romans*, 13:14.
12. Tweedie, pp. 364-365.
13. Joseph Campbell, *The Hero with a Thousand Faces*, p. 39.
14. Ghalib, trans. Jane Hirshfield, *The Enlightened Heart*, ed. Stephen Mitchell, p. 103.
15. Tweedie, p. 466.

The Inner Feminine and Her Dual Nature

1. *Song of Songs*, 6:10.
2. Hâfiz, in Nurbakhsh, *Sufi Symbolism*, vol. 1, p. 6.
3. Keats, "La Belle Dame sans Merci," x-xi.

4. Recorded by Suzanne Percheron, in *C. G. Jung, Emma Jung, and Toni Wolff: A Collection of Remembrances*, p. 53.

5. Jung, *Collected Works*, vol. 14, para. 216.

6. Shakespeare, *Hamlet*, III.iv. 91-94.

7. Erich Neumann, *The Origins and History of Consciousness*, p. 85.

8. *Hamlet*, V.i. 281-283.

9. In *The Acts of Thomas* there is a Eucharistic prayer which uses similar imagery to worship the Holy Ghost in its feminine form:

> Come holy dove,
> Which hast brought forth the twin nestlings;
> Come secret mother...

quoted by Jung, *Collected Works*, vol. 5, para. 561.

10. Jung, *Memories, Dreams, Reflections*, p. 212.

11. Jung, *Memories, Dreams, Reflections*, p. 212.

12. Marie-Louise von Franz, *The Way of the Dream*, p. 268.

13. J. C. Cooper, *An Illustrated Encyclopedia of Traditional Symbols*, p.14.

14. Jung, *Collected Works*, vol. 9ii, para. 24.

15. Quoted by Laleh Bakhtiar in *Sufi Expressions of the Mystic Quest*, p. 21.

16. See Nurbakhsh, *Sufi Symbolism*, vol. 1.

17. Hâfiz, in *Sufi Symbolism*, vol. 1, p. 23.

18. *Song of Songs*, 4:12-16.

19. Tweedie, quoted by Roger Housden in *The Fire in the Heart*, p. 164.

20. John Donne, "Batter my Heart, three person'd God."

21. Kabir, *Songs of Kabir*, trans. R. Tagore, XVII.

22. Huston Smith, *Beyond the Post-Modern Mind*, pp. 111-112.

23. *King Lear*, ed. K. Muir, V.iii. 16-17.

24. Ibn 'Arabî, quoted by Corbin in *Creative Imagination in the Sufism of Ibn 'Arabi*, pp. 174-175.

The Unattainable Bride

1. *Song of Songs*, 4:9.

2. Qur'an, 5:59, quoted by A. J. Arberry in *The Doctrine of the Sufis*, p. 155.

3. Rûmî, "Eight," in *Rumi, Fragments, Ecstasies*, trans. Daniel Liebert.

4. Tweedie, pp. 634-635.

5. Diane Wolkenstein and S. N. Kramer, *Inanna: Queen of Heaven and Earth*, p. 37.

6. Jung notes:

> There are certain types of women who seem to be made by nature to attract anima projections; indeed one could almost speak of a definite "anima type." The so-called "sphinx-like" character is an indispensable part of their equipment, also an equivocalness, an intriguing elusiveness... an indefinableness that seems full of promises, like the speaking silence of the Mona Lisa. A woman of this kind is both old and young, mother and daughter, of a more than doubtful chastity, childlike and yet endowed with a naive cunning that is extremely disarming to men *(Collected Works*,vol. 17, para. 339).

7. Kabir, *Songs of Kabir*, trans. R. Tagore, XLVII.

8. Robert Johnson, *The Psychology of Romantic Love*, p. xiii. Possibly the animus and anima have become more differentiated in the Western psyche.

9. *I Corinthians*, 13:4-7.

10. Qur'an, 50:16.

11. Jâmî, *Yusuf and Zulaikha*, trans. David Pendlebury, p. 6.

12. Qur'an, 20:43, quoted by Arberry, p. 113.

13. Jâmî, p. 15.

14. Jâmî, p. 17.

15. e.e. cummings, "yes is a pleasant country," *Selected Poems*, p. 64.

16. Jâmî, p. 56.

17. Jâmî, p. 57.

18. Rûmî, *Open Secret*, p. 82.
19. Fynn, *Mister God, This is Anna*, p. 179.
20. Jâmî, p. 107.
21. Jâmî, p. 119.
22. Ahmad Ghazzâlî, *Sawânih*, trans. Nasrollah Pourjavady, p. 92.
23. Jâmî, p. 145.
24. Nizami, *The Story of Layla & Majnun*, trans. R. Gelpke, p. 29.
25. Nizami, p. 37.
26. Tweedie, p. 551.
27. Tweedie, p. 552.
28. Nicholson, *Studies in Islamic Mysticism*, p. 55.
29. Nizami, p. 44.
30. Nizami, p. 126.
31. St. John of the Cross, *Ascent of Mount Carmel*, 1:13.
32. Nizami, p. 195.
33. Quoted by Nicholson in *Studies in Islamic Mysticism*, p. 80.

The Alchemical Opus III: Symbols of the Self

1. Miguel Serrano, *C. G. Jung and Herman Hesse*, p. 60.
2. *Katha Upanishad*, trans. Shree Purohit Swâmi and W. B. Yeats, bk. II, 1.
3. *Man and His Symbols*, ed. Jung, p. 209.
4. *Man and His Symbols*, p. 207.
5. Jung, *Collected Works*, vol. 9ii, para. 231.
6. Jung continually oriented his work away from the vagaries of mysticism towards *this* world: "I aimed, after all, at *this* world, and *this* life. I always knew that everything I was experiencing was ultimately directed at this real life of mine" (*Memories, Dreams, Reflections*, p. 214).
7. Quoted by Louis Massignon, *The Passion of al-Hallâj*, vol. 1, p. 285.
8. *St. Matthew*, 8:20.

9. Rûmî, trans. Andrew Harvey, *Light Upon Light*, p. 39.
10. Jung, *Collected Works*, vol. 9i, para. 646.
11. Andrew Samuels, *A Critical Dictionary of Jungian Analysis*, p. 150.
12. Lâhîjî, quoted by Corbin, *The Man of Light in Iranian Sufism*, p. 118.
13. Rûmî, "The Truth Within Us," *Rumi, Poet and Mystic*, trans. R. A. Nicholson, p. 47.
14. *The Revelation of St. John the Divine*, 21:10-23.
15. Quoted by Corbin, *The Man of Light in Iranian Sufism*, p. 72.
16. Jacobi, *The Way of Individuation*, pp. 108-109.

The Relationship with the Teacher

1. Tweedie, p. 87.
2. Irina Tweedie, New Dimensions radio interview, June 1987.
3. *Mathnawî*, I, 2943-2945, quoted by Eva de Vitray-Meyerovitch in *Rumi and Sufism*, p. 117.
4. Nurbakhsh, p. 201.
5. 'Attâr, trans. Nurbakhsh, p. 208.
6. Najmuddîn Kubrâ, quoted by Corbin in *The Man of Light in Iranian Sufism*, p. 72.
7. Psalm 36:9.
8. Kubrâ, quoted by Corbin in *The Man of Light in Iranian Sufism*, p. 73.
9. Corbin, *The Man of Light in Iranian Sufism*, p. 73.
10. Tweedie, p. 280.
11. Tweedie, p. 222.
12. Tweedie, p. 404.
13. Abû Sa'îd of Mihneh, quoted by Rice in *The Persian Sufis*, pp. 33-34.
14. Quoted by Alexander Lipski, *Life and Teaching of Anandamayi Ma*, p. 50.
15. Quoted by J. G. Bennett in *The Masters of Wisdom*, p. 180.
16. Tweedie, p. 120.

17. Tweedie, p. 120.
18. Anandamayi Ma, quoted by Lipski, p. 50.
19. Unpublished quotation by Irina Tweedie.
20. Nicholson, *The Mystics of Islam*, p. 31.
21. Quoted by Anne Bancroft, *Weavers of Wisdom*, p. 67.
22. One friend had a dream in which the teacher is a shopkeeper offering the dreamer whatever she wants. This dream suggests that it is important for the dreamer to decide what she wants, and although the teacher does not ask any money, the dreamer is aware that "the things are not free." She must pay with herself. (See Vaughan-Lee, *The Lover and the Serpent*, pp. 117-120.)
23. Quoted by Bennett, p. 180.
24. Tweedie, p. 529.
25. 'Attâr, *Muslim Saints and Mystics*, p. 121.
26. Ghazzâlî, *Sawânih*, p. 66.
27. *Al-Anwar al-Kudsiva* (The Divine Lights of the Naqshbandi Path), private trans. See also Hasan Shushud, *The Masters of Wisdom of Central Asia*, p. 44.
28. Tweedie, "Tested with Fire and Spirit," unreleased video interview, June 1988.
29. The Blessed John Ruysbroeck, *Adornment of the Spiritual Marriage*, trans. C. A. Wynschenck Dom, p. 171.

The Poverty of the Heart

1. Rûmî, trans. John Moyne and Coleman Barks, *Open Secret*, p. 47.
2. Idries Shah, *Thinkers of the East*, p. 145.
3. Quoted by Sara Sviri, "The Naqshbandi Path," unpublished lecture.
4. Joseph Campbell, *The Power of Myth*, p. 89.
5. The Blessed John Ruysbroeck, *Adornment of the Spiritual Marriage*, III:4.
6. *St. Matthew*, 5:3.
7. *St. Matthew*, 7:14.
8. Sermon: "Blessed are the Poor."
9. *St. Matthew*, 19:14.

10. William Blake "Nurse's Song," ll. 1-4.
11. *St. Matthew*, 6:28-29. See also above, p. 26.
12. Lâhîjî, quoted by Corbin in *The Man of Light in Iranian Sufism*, p. 118.
13. Jung, *Memories, Dreams, Reflections*, p. 355.
14. *St. John*, 10:30.
15. Idries Shah, *The Way of the Sufi*, p. 156.
16. Quoted from "Mother Teresa Sees Herself as God's Pencil," The Tribune News Services (date unknown).
17. Rûmî, trans. John Moyne and Coleman Barks, *Open Secret*, p. 21.
18. Tweedie, p. 387.
19. *The Revelation of St. John the Divine*, 22:1.
20. Tweedie, p. 165.
21. St. Catherine of Genoa, quoted in *Silent Fire: An Invitation to Western Mysticism*, eds. Walter Holden Capps and Wendy M. Wright.
22. 'Attâr, *The Conference of the Birds*, p. 119.
23. Tweedie, p. 728.
24. Arguelles, p. 99.

SELECTED BIBLIOGRAPHY

Arguelles, Miriam and Jose. *The Feminine.* Boulder: Shambhala Publications, 1977.

Arberry, Arthur J. *The Doctrine of the Sufis.* Lahore: Sh. Muhammad Ashraf, 1966.

'Attâr, Farîd ud-Dîn. *The Conference of the Birds.* Trans. C. S. Nott. London: Routledge & Kegan Paul, 1961.

—. *Muslim Saints and Mystics.* Trans. A. J. Arberry. London: Routledge & Kegan Paul, 1966.

Bakhtiar, Laleh. *Sufi Expressions of the Mystic Quest.* London: Thames and Hudson, 1976.

Bancroft, Anne. *Weavers of Wisdom: Women Mystics of the Twentieth Century.* London: Arkana, 1989.

Bennett, J. G. *The Masters of Wisdom.* London: Turnstone Press, 1977.

Bhatnagar, R. S. *Dimensions of Classical Sufi Thought.* London and The Hague: East West Publications, 1984.

Blake, William. *Complete Writings.* Ed. Geoffrey Keynes. Oxford: Oxford University Press, 1969.

Bly, Robert. *A Little Book on the Human Shadow.* San Francisco: Harper and Row, 1988.

Campbell, Joseph. *The Hero With a Thousand Faces.* London: Abacus, 1975.

—. *The Power of Myth.* London: Doubleday, 1989.

Capps, Walter Holden and Wright, Wendy M., eds. *Silent Fire: An Invitation to Western Mysticism.* San Francisco: Harper & Row, 1978.

Castillejo, Irene de. *Knowing Woman.* New York: Harper Colophon, 1974.

Cirlot, J. E. *A Dictionary of Symbols.* London: Routledge & Kegan Paul, 1962.

Cooper, J. C. *An Illustrated Encyclopedia of Traditional Symbols.* London: Thames and Hudson, 1978.

Corbin, Henry. *Creative Imagination in the Sufism of Ibn 'Arabi.* Princeton: Princeton University Press, 1969.

—. *The Man of Light in Iranian Sufism.* London: Shambhala, 1978.
—. *Spiritual Body and Celestial Earth.* London: I. B. Tauris, 1990.
cummings, e. e. *Selected Poems.* London: Faber and Faber, 1960.
Donne, John. *Complete Poetry and Selected Prose.* London: The Nonesuch Press, 1972.
Eckhart. *Meister Eckhart.* Trans. R. Blakney. New York: Harper and Row, 1951.
Edinger, Edward. *The Anatomy of the Psyche.* La Salle: Open Court, 1985.
Eliot, T. S. *Collected Poems.* London: Faber and Faber, 1963.
Fynn. *Mister God, This is Anna.* London: Collins, 1974.
Ghazzali, Ahmad. *Sawânih: Inspiration from the World of Pure Spirits.* Trans. Nasrollah Pourjavady. London: Routledge & Kegan Paul, 1986.
Happold, F. C. *Mysticism.* Harmondsworth: Penguin Books, 1963.
Harding, M. Esther. *Woman's Mysteries.* London: Rider & Co., 1971.
Holy Bible, King James Version.
Housden, Roger. *The Fire in the Heart.* Shaftesbury: Element Books, 1990.
Jacobi, Jolande. *The Way of Individuation.* New York: Harcourt Brace and World, 1967.
Jâmî. *Yusuf and Zulaikha.* Trans. David Pendlebury. London: Octagon Press, 1980.
Jensen, Ferne, ed. *C. G. Jung, Emma Jung, and Toni Wolff: A Collection of Remembrances.* San Francisco: The Analytical Psychology Club of San Francisco, 1982.
Johnson, Robert. *The Psychology of Romantic Love.* London: Routledge & Kegan Paul, 1984.
Jump, John, ed. *Shakespeare: Hamlet, A Casebook.* Nashville: Aurora, 1970.
Jung, C. G. *Collected Letters.* 2 vols. London: Routledge & Kegan Paul, 1973 & 1976.
—. *Collected Works.* London: Routledge & Kegan Paul.
—, ed. *Man and His Symbols.* London: Aldus Books, 1964.

—. *Memories, Dreams, Reflections.* London: Flamingo, 1983.

—. *The Psychology of the Transference.* London: Arc Paperbacks, 1983.

—. *Word and Image.* Princeton: Princeton University Press, 1979.

Kabir. *Songs of Kabir.* Trans. R. Tagore. New York: Samuel Weiser, 1915.

Keats, John. *Poetical Works.* Oxford: Oxford University Press, 1956.

Koran. Trans. N. J. Dawood. London: Penguin Books, 1956.

Lipski, Alexander. *Life and Teaching of Anandamayi Ma.* Delhi: Motilal Banarsidass, 1979.

Massignon, Louis. *The Passion of al-Hallâj.* 2 vols. Princeton: Princeton University Press, 1982.

Miller, Alice. *The Drama of the Gifted Child.* London: Virago, 1987.

Mitchell, Stephen, ed. *The Enlightened Heart.* New York: Harper and Row, 1989.

—, trans. *Tao Te Ching.* New York: Harper and Row, 1989.

Neumann, Erich. *The Origins and History of Consciousness.* Princeton: Princeton University Press, 1970.

—. "The Psychological Stages of Feminine Development." In *Spring,* 1957, pp. 63-97.

Nichols, Sallie. *Jung and Tarot, An Archetypal Journey.* Maine: Samuel Weiser, 1980.

Nicholson, R. A. *The Mystics of Islam.* London: Arkana, 1989.

—. *Studies in Islamic Mysticism.* Cambridge: Cambridge University Press, 1921.

Nizami. *The Story of Layla & Majnun.* Trans. R. Gelpke. London: Bruno Cassirer, 1966.

Nurbakhsh, J. *Sufi Symbolism.* London: Khaniqahi-Nimatullahi Publications, 1984.

Pendlebury, David, trans. *Four Sufi Classics.* London: Octagon Press, 1982.

Qualls-Corbett, Nancy. *The Sacred Prostitute.* Toronto: Inner City Books, 1988.

Rabi'a. *Doorkeeper of the Heart.* Trans. Charles Upton. Putney, Vermont: Threshold Books, 1988.

Rice, Cyprian. *The Persian Sufis.* London: George Allen & Unwin, 1964.
Rûmî. *Light Upon Light.* Trans. Andrew Harvey. Berkeley: North Atlantic Books, 1996.
—. *Open Secret: Versions of Rumi.* Trans. John Moyne and Coleman Barks. Putney, Vermont: Threshold Books, 1984.
—. *Rumi, Fragments, Ecstasies.* Trans. Daniel Liebert. Santa Fe: Source Books, 1981.
—. *Rumi, Poet and Mystic.* Trans. R. A. Nicholson. Northampton: John Dickens & Company, 1950.
Ruysbroeck, The Blessed John. *Adornment of the Spiritual Marriage.* London: Dent, 1916.
Samuels, Andrew. *A Critical Dictionary of Jungian Analysis.* London: Routledge & Kegan Paul, 1986.
Schimmel, Annemarie. *Pain and Grace.* Leiden: E. J. Brill, 1976.
Schreiner, Olive. *Dreams.* London: Wildwood House, 1982.
Serrano, Miguel. *C. G. Jung and Herman Hesse, A Record of Two Friendships.* London: Routledge & Kegan Paul, 1986.
Shah, Idries. *The Way of the Sufi.* Harmondsworth: Penguin Books, 1974.
—. *Thinkers of the East.* Baltimore, Maryland: Penguin Books, 1972.
Shakespeare, *Hamlet.* Ed. Harold Jenkins. London: Methuen & Co., 1982.
—. *King Lear.* Ed. Kenneth Muir. London: Methuen & Co., 1952.
Shushud, Hasan. *The Masters of Wisdom of Central Asia.* Trans. Muhtar Holland. Ellingstring: Coombe Spring Press, 1983.
Smith, Huston. *Beyond the Post-Modern Mind.* New York: Harper Colophon Books, 1977.
Spiegelman, J. Marvin, ed. *Sufism, Islam and Jungian Psychology.* Scottsdale, Arizona: New Falcon Publications, 1991.
St. John of the Cross. *Ascent of Mount Carmel.* Garden City, New York: Image Books, 1958.

Tagore, Rabindranath. *Collected Poems and Plays of Rabindranath Tagore.* London: Macmillan, 1936.

Thompson, Francis. "The Hound of Heaven." In *Oxford Book of Mystical Verse.* Oxford: Clarenden Press, 1917.

Tweedie, Irina. *Daughter of Fire: A Diary of a Spiritual Training with a Sufi Master.* Inverness, California: The Golden Sufi Center, 1986.

Vaughan-Lee, Llewellyn. *The Lover and the Serpent.* Shaftesbury: Element Books, 1990.

Vitray-Meyerovitch, Eva de. *Rumi and Sufism.* Sausalito, California: The Post-Apollo Press, 1987.

von Franz, Marie-Louise. *Jung, His Myth in Our Time.* New York: C. G. Jung Foundation, 1975.

—. *The Way of the Dream.* Toronto: Windrose Films Ltd., 1988.

Wilson, Peter Lamborn and Pourjavady, Nasrollah. *The Drunken Universe.* Grand Rapids: Phanes Press, 1987.

Wolkenstein, Diane and Kramer, S. N. *Inanna: Queen of Heaven and Earth.* New York: Harper and Row, 1983.

Wordsworth, William. *Poetical Works.* London: Oxford University Press, 1936.

Yeats, W. B., trans. (with Shree Purohit Swami). *The Ten Principal Upanishads.* London: Faber and Faber, 1937.

INDEX

ACKNOWLEDGMENTS

For permission to use copyright material, the author gratefully wishes to acknowledge: Daniel Liebert for permission to quote from *Rumi: Fragments, Ecstasies*, translated by Daniel Liebert; HarperCollins Publishers for permission to quote four lines from *Tao Te Ching by Lao Tzu: A New English Version*, with forward and notes by Stephen Mitchell, translation copyright ©1988 by Stephen Mitchell; Jane Hirshfield for permission to quote lines from "The world is no more than the Beloved's single face" and "Before there was a trace of this world of men," which appear in *The Enlightened Heart: An Anthology of Sacred Poetry*, edited by Stephen Mitchell, copyright ©1989 by Jane Hirshfield; Khaniqahi Nimatullahi Publications for permission to quote from *Sufi Symbolism: Volume One*, by Dr. Javad Nurbakhsh; Andrew Harvey for permission to quote from *Light Upon Light: Inspirations from Rumi*, by Andrew Harvey, copyright ©1996 by Andrew Harvey, used by permission of North Atlantic Books, Berkeley, California; Omega Publications for permission to quote from *The Drunken Universe*, translated by Peter Lamborn Wilson and Nasrollah Pourjavady; Henry Corbin, *Creative Imagination in the Sufism of Ibn 'Arabî*, copyright Princeton University Press, reprinted by permission; Threshold Books for permission to quote from *Open Secret: Versions of Rumi*, translated by John Moyne and Coleman Barks, and also for permission to quote from *Doorkeeper of the Heart: Versions of Râbi'a*, translated by Charles Upton.

LLEWELLYN VAUGHAN-LEE, Ph.D., was born in London in 1953 and has followed the Sufi path since he was nineteen. In 1991 he moved with his family to Northern California and founded The Golden Sufi Center (www.goldensufi.org).

Author of several books, he has specialized in the area of dreamwork, integrating the ancient Sufi approach to dreams with the insights of modern psychology. Since 2000 the focus of his writing and teaching has been on spiritual responsibility in our present time of transition, an awakening global consciousness of oneness, and spiritual ecology (www.workingwithoneness.org). He has been interviewed by Oprah Winfrey on *Super Soul Sunday*, and featured on the *Global Spirit* series shown on PBS.

THE GOLDEN SUFI CENTER is a 501(c)(3) California Religious Non-Profit Corporation dedicated to making the teachings of the Naqshbandi Sufi Path available to all seekers. For further information about the activities of the Center please contact us at:

THE GOLDEN SUFI CENTER
P.O. Box 456
Point Reyes, California 94956
tel: (415) 663-0100 · *fax:* (415) 663-0103
www.goldensufi.org